The Data Path
Less Traveled

Step up Creativity using Heuristics in
Data Science, Artificial Intelligence, and Beyond

Zacharias Voulgaris, PhD

Technics Publications

115 Linda Vista, Sedona, AZ 86336 USA
https://www.TechnicsPub.com

Cover design by Lorena Molinari
Edited by Jamie Hoberman

First Edition
First Printing 2022
Copyright © 2022 Zacharias Voulgaris, PhD

ISBN, print ed.   9781634628570
ISBN, Kindle ed.   9781634628587
ISBN, PDF ed.   9781634628600
ISBN, ePub ed.   9781634628594

Library of Congress Control Number: 2022936565

*Dedicated to all those who have developed their own heuristics
and used them for data-related pursuits*

Contents

Introduction

This book uses a hands-on approach to explain creativity via heuristics within analytics, data science, and artificial intelligence (AI). Each of the five parts within these pages contains chapters that explore heuristics and their application to solving problems.

Solving problems is essential in any analytics project. Often these problems require extra attention since there isn't always an algorithm or some formula that will yield a viable solution. Besides, problem-solving is a soft skill that's part of the job description (at least in those cases where the hiring manager is honest about the position and what it entails). But solving problems can be time-consuming and sometimes not feasible within the resource budget at hand. So, getting some help with it wouldn't hurt, and it could save everyone some time, which we can better spend on other tasks.

Heuristics can provide such help, particularly when it comes to data-related problems. These don't have to do with hard-core analytics work per se since sometimes we just need to optimize a mathematical function or a process that would otherwise be a bottleneck in our pipeline. Heuristics have us covered in those cases too! But unlike other metrics and methods we encounter in data science and AI, heuristics require some work from us too, a sense of creativity. Combined with an engineering mindset that thrives on such challenges and finds down-to-earth solutions for them, heuristics can be a valuable asset that can add value to us both as analytics professionals and problem-solvers.

Part I provides an overview of heuristics and covers each of the various types of heuristics. Part II focuses on data-oriented heuristics and how they apply specifically to data science problems. Part III explains optimization-oriented heuristics and how they solve challenging optimization problems. Part IV is all about designing and implementing your own heuristics to help with particular problems. Finally, Part V contains additional topics on heuristics, such as transparency and limitations.

Chapter summaries reinforce the key points of each chapter, a glossary explains important terms within our field, and several appendices contain reference material on heuristics and related programming tools. In addition, several chapters illustrate material with a code notebook (.jl files) in the Julia language. Download all the notebooks at https://technicspub.com/TheDataPathLessTraveled.

Probably you are itching to learn more about this fascinating subject, so without any further ado, let's get started!

PART I

About Heuristics

A heuristic is simply a guideline or a rough-and-ready rule to solve a particular type of problem.

Shailesh Shirali

CHAPTER 1

Creative Problem-solving

1.1 Problem-solving

After getting down the basics of data science or data analytics, a learner of the craft needs to dig deeper. After all, we aren't paid for the knowledge we have in our field, but for the problems we are capable of solving. Perhaps that's why problem-solving is a highly valued skill in data science. We must solve both complex and challenging problems.

Naturally, this problem-solving skill becomes even more relevant when dealing with problems that require more than just crunching numbers. For example, many processes in an organization today involve optimization. Optimization is all about finding the best solution. This solution can be a value or a set of values that maximize or minimize a given metric. So, in this case, problem-solving is all about optimizing effectively and efficiently. Unfortunately, that's not as easy as it sounds! These processes often involve many variables, making the search space vast and impossible to manage with basic optimization methods.

Of course, problem-solving includes other techniques, such as figuring out a viable strategy in a more abstract setting. For example, deciding which tools to use and how to achieve a given objective within a given time frame. Although these sorts of problems are more challenging to formulate and resolve, the right auxiliary tools can simplify the problems or enable us to view them from a different perspective. Fortunately, these tools are known, at least to some extent, and you can learn them to some level of proficiency. Unfortunately, they aren't easy to master, particularly if you aspire to make the most out of them. For lack of a better term, we can call these tools *heuristics*, even if that implies a relatively limited scope. Problem-solving isn't a skill you can master easily, but more of an aptitude you constantly refine. Heuristics can help a great deal in problem-solving, especially in the beginning.

It's best to know the basics of the craft first since heuristics require them. This knowledge of the basics is like Lego blocks, with which you can design and construct more elaborate structures. Heuristics are the mental shortcuts that enable you to make headway in the practically infinite complexity of these elaborate structures. As a bonus, they make the whole journey more enjoyable as they highlight the presence of something beyond rigid rules and established paths, honing your creative abilities and intuition.

1.2 Creativity in problem-solving

Creativity is a very broad skill that applies in various aspects of the data science craft. It is what enables you to explore new possibilities and, more practically, new solutions to a given problem or task. That's one of the reasons it's inherently linked to problem-solving, more so than any other soft skill in this field. How many times have you heard the term "creative solution" concerning a tricky problem?

Creativity in problem-solving is all about exploring the solution space in an intelligent manner that's also quite efficient. It often involves leveraging some understanding of the problem that helps you traverse the solution space faster and more intelligently. However, automating all this isn't easy and often requires a novel approach (strategy). Not all novel approaches work, however, and if you were to pick a strategy at random, the chances are that it wouldn't work all that well. Nevertheless, exploring pathways to the solution you haven't explored before is possible if you leverage randomness. That's not to say that you would be flipping coins to solve a problem, but if you were to express this whole process so a computer could understand, randomness could be a useful tool.

Trial-and-error is an alternative to randomness, and it leaves a lot of the guesswork out when it comes to designing a metric or a method for solving the problem. Once you have defined the problem mathematically (to the best extent this is possible), you can develop a tool to help you gauge your progress, perhaps a set of rules-of-thumb that can guide you to the required solution. Then, by trying various ways, you can gradually build a heuristic that will make the whole process more manageable and easier to understand. So, in a way, heuristics can be an expression of creativity, an expression that would work for problem-solving at least.

Note that creativity can work in many problem-solving scenarios, not just the more challenging ones. In fact, it's usually better to try it out on a simpler version of the problem at hand and gradually make the problem tougher. As this happens, you can refine your understanding of the problem and therefore refine your heuristic, gradually honing your problem-solving strategy. After all, the best way to solve a problem is to become better at solving problems. Heuristics can be an invaluable aid.

The more you work with heuristics, the better you become at using them to tackle whatever problem comes your way, at least in data- and optimization-related scenarios.

1.3 AI and creativity

Artificial intelligence requires creativity as well. After all, AI has impressed many people with its variety of applications and its creative solutions to complex problems across different domains. It's even made strides in design tasks, which until then, were thought to be something only humans could handle, at least in a creative fashion.

Of course, AI handles creativity completely differently, as the diagram in Fig. 1.1 illustrates. Still, it works and is very applicable, so creative AI systems must be doing something right!

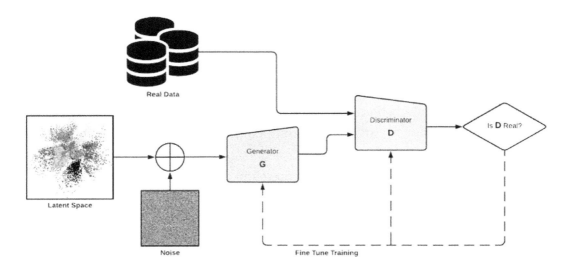

Fig. 1.1 A diagram of how creativity comes about in an AI setting, based on the work of I. J. Goodfellow and his team (2014). It may not be as interesting as the creativity we experience, but that's how computers understand and express it.

AI performs creative tasks by leveraging randomness to create new points in the solution space (i.e., new solutions). Then, it checks each solution to see if it's "real" enough (i.e., a valid option). It repeats this process several times until more realistic solutions come about. Since the solution space can be anything (it's all ones and zeros as far as the computer is concerned), these solutions can apply to any problem. The only requirement is that the problem be well-defined and expressed numerically.

This simple requirement makes the solution space a finite entity (though quite a vast one) and the solution viable in an algorithmic way. Frequently, the solution space entails several dimensions, making the whole process quite demanding in terms of resources. After all, AI doesn't just come up with solutions but "learns" from this whole process to replicate other, similar solutions at will. In other words, it develops a mapping of sorts, linking the realistic solutions to the inputs, so it "knows" which combinations of variable values (values in the solution space) yield a good enough solution.

But how does AI know how to evaluate a solution? Well, that's where the human user comes in. After all, learning is not possible in a vacuum. This knowledge needs to come from somewhere. In some cases, where the environment is well-defined, as in the case of a game, this knowledge may derive from the feedback the game gives to AI—for example, the points gained or a winning outcome. What if the whole process was reversed, though, so that there wasn't any AI present and it was just you against the problem, with a computer helping you out? That's where heuristics would enter the picture in a very practical and hands-on way.

1.4 Down-to-earth creativity

But how exactly can we leverage creativity in problem-solving? Well, that's where *down-to-earth creativity* comes in. Although this isn't an official term, it does distinguish this kind of creativity from more abstract creativity, often employed in other, more artistic areas. Besides, in data science, we need to be quite down-to-earth and hands-on, if we are to offer any value.

Down-to-earth creativity is essentially creativity applied to problem-solving. Creative problem-solving involves tackling and providing adequate solutions to data science and optimization-related problems. Why adequate solutions? When we are being pragmatic in solving a problem, we cannot afford to opt for the best theoretical solutions because they are often inaccessible. In other words, it would require a tremendous amount of computational resources to find these "perfect" solutions. In contrast, other solutions which are just good enough may be a better choice as they are better value for the money. Fortunately, heuristics can help us in this immensely.

Creative problem-solving doesn't involve heuristics only, however. It is a mindset of sorts that involves the use of imagination and coming up with novel ideas. Heuristics can be a great tool to develop this mindset. The more you use them, the better you understand them and the wider your perception becomes.

Additionally, you may create your own heuristics that lead to better solutions and refine your problem-solving abilities.

Domain knowledge is always invaluable in our work and in solving problems we encounter. After all, there is a reason why subject matter experts (SMEs) are sought after when dealing with complex projects. Domain knowledge deepens our understanding of the problem and helps us develop more relevant solutions. Much like evaluating how "real" a solution is in the AI approach to the problem, the SME can provide us with the essential feedback that can help us refine our course through the solution space.

1.5 Summary

From all this, it's clear that creative problem-solving is a multi-faceted matter that requires both imagination and a down-to-earth understanding of what's happening in a particular domain. But if we are to solve a problem effectively, we need to leverage some shortcuts and rules of thumb. Often heuristics can manifest these and help us tackle a problem in a data-driven manner that can be much faster and more cost-effective.

CHAPTER 2

What Are Heuristics?

2.1 Heuristics overview

Let's start this heuristics journey by looking broadly at heuristics across data science and AI.

A heuristic is an empirical method or algorithm that provides a useful tool or insight to facilitate the method or project.

The latter can be related to data science, AI, or both. Note that I fashioned this definition for technical disciplines like ours. In psychology, for example, it has a somewhat different meaning, namely, a kind of mental shortcut or rule of thumb to facilitate reasoning.

Note that a heuristic can take the form of a function that you can implement as an auxiliary script, if you prefer. This approach is often a practical way to manifest the heuristic using a programming language of your choice. Even though any data science language would do, we'll use Julia in this book because of its efficiency and ease of use.

Additionally, heuristics are entirely data-driven and focus on performing a specific task efficiently and scalable. Keep that in mind, as it's a good heuristic (in the psychological sense of the word) for discerning what metrics and methods qualify as heuristics and what don't!

The fact that heuristics aren't well-known shouldn't dissuade you from leveraging them. After all, it's a bit of a niche topic in data science and AI, even if it's a popular research avenue. Still, they are growing in popularity, and you may find yourself using them already, to some extent, without even knowing. Keep an open mind about heuristics and expand on the topic when you get the basics down.

It's useful to think of a heuristic as a computationally light method that yields a result that can save you time and computational resources. The result that a heuristic yields may not always be accurate, but it is a good approximation of the required solution and sometimes the only accessible solution. Naturally, you can't base a whole analysis on heuristics, but you can rely on them extensively for understanding the data better and approximating a solution to a data-related problem.

This chapter will explore heuristics as metrics and algorithms and examine some important considerations. This can lay the foundations for the chapters that follow, where we'll look at heuristics in more detail and, in particular, applications related to both data science and AI. Feel free to consult the glossary if you need more information on any heuristics terms. Also, consider specific examples in your work or experience where this information applies. This can help cement what's described here and make it your own.

2.2 Heuristics as metrics

Heuristics as metrics are an ideal option for modern data science work since they are the best of both worlds, combining conventional analytics with data-driven analysis. In fact, it is the cornerstone of the data-driven paradigm, while at the same time, they borrow a lot from the model-driven paradigm underlying conventional analytics.

However, heuristics as metrics are not supported by theory. They are just methods that work for a particular problem and measure what we need to gauge. That is what makes them relatively easy to apply. A heuristic metric is a powerful tool, but only when applied to problems relevant to that metric in terms of scope, which we'll cover later in this book.

Additionally, heuristics as metrics are the most obvious application of these tools, even if many people take them for granted. There are a few well-known heuristic metrics, such as the F1 score for assessing classifier performance in relation to a given class, or the various similarity metrics that show us the similarity between two data points. These metrics are quite popular, and people don't really think about them very much because of their frequent use. That's why they often don't even use the term *heuristics* to describe them.

Heuristics as metrics are commonly used in data science work, though they aren't limited to data science. Still, it makes more sense to use them with actual data than with the outputs of arbitrary functions, as in abstract AI applications such as optimization. In any case, they can be very valuable and, in some cases, a flexible tool. Of course, their flexibility depends on how well you know them and your skills as a problem-solver.

Although heuristic metrics are somewhat similar to conventional statistics, they are a very powerful tool in the data-driven paradigm. So whenever you're using machine learning and machine learning-related methods, you will have to deal with heuristics in one way or another.

Since heuristics are underused, there is much untapped potential. Heuristics as metrics, in particular, have a lot of room for growth and evolution.

2.3 Heuristics as algorithms

Heuristics as algorithms are more popular than heuristics as metrics, at least for mainstream data science and AI. This is because heuristics as algorithms have been around longer, and therefore, there are many applications in both of these fields. In fact, it is likely that AI would have never evolved much without the use of algorithm-related heuristics. The same goes for data-driven data science (particularly machine learning), which relies greatly on some of these heuristics-based methods.

What's more, heuristics as algorithms are ideal for complex problems. Such problems may involve high dimensionality, many restrictions, or anything that would require a lot of computational power to handle analytically. Perhaps that's why heuristics algorithms are particularly useful for optimization problems and AI in general, even though this kind of heuristic can apply to all sorts of scenarios involving processes. In all cases, a heuristics algorithm needs to be relatively flexible and scalable for the heuristic to be useful.

For example, you can use a heuristics as algorithms approach to find the best variables to use in a data set for feature engineering and other scenarios where you deal with Natural Processing Processing (NP) problems. You can even view the common clustering algorithms used today as this type of heuristic algorithm. Also, because heuristics algorithms are ingrained in our understanding of the data-driven approach, many people incorrectly think of this type of heuristic when they hear this term. However, in academia, where people are more aligned with this way of thinking, the term heuristic has a very particular meaning in this kind of work, usually related to metrics and methods for facilitating the solution of a complex problem.

Heuristics as algorithms are a more challenging area and require a good understanding of the problem. Maybe that's why most practitioners do not choose them when figuring out the solution to a new problem. After all, developing a new heuristic is not a simple matter, as we'll discuss shortly. Still, it's often necessary, especially when the problem is too difficult or too computationally expensive to solve otherwise.

Just like in other kinds of heuristics, heuristics as algorithms has a great deal of untapped potential, especially with research. So there are lots of theoretical methods in the research sector. For example, when it comes to optimization, new algorithmic heuristics often make their way to papers as potential ways to tackle very challenging problems.

2.4 Important considerations

There are some important considerations when it comes to heuristics. First of all, heuristics as metrics may be new to you, and therefore there is a learning curve. Still, a couple of heuristic metrics are more or less mainstream, so this can be a good starting point for you. We'll cover them later in this book.

Also, heuristics are not a panacea, even if they are powerful tools to express creativity. They have a lot of potential and a lot of application possibilities making your problem-solving efforts much easier, but they can't solve every single problem. Even if a heuristic could potentially solve a very challenging problem, it doesn't mean that it is always available. Perhaps they need some refinement or alternation, something you would probably have to do yourself.

Additionally, algorithm-related heuristics can have lots of variants. On the other hand, very few metrics-related heuristics follow this pattern. This is because algorithm-related heuristics have been around longer. So they can branch out in different variations to solve a problem differently and sometimes more efficiently, since the problems they tackle are often broader and offer themselves different approaches for finding a solution, such as with multi-variate optimization problems.

Also, the usefulness of a heuristic depends on your knowledge of how to leverage it to the problem at hand. A heuristic may be very powerful, but if you don't understand how it works and what parameters need tweaking (remember, creativity!), it may not yield the expected results. Even with available documentation, heuristics can be hard to master, especially for complex problems. Perhaps that's why heuristics aren't as popular as other parts of data science and AI.

Despite these considerations and many more that we will cover in this book, heuristics are very hands-on and practical.

2.5 Summary

We explained heuristics and their important considerations. We saw that heuristics are metrics or algorithms and are usually expressed as programming functions or auxiliary scripts.

Heuristics as metrics are cornerstones of the data-driven paradigm and therefore particularly applicable in data science problems. Heuristics as algorithms useful for AI-related problems and complex problems in general. As a general rule, problems that are too computationally expensive to solve analytically lend themselves to heuristics.

Remember that the usefulness of a heuristic depends on your knowledge of how to leverage it to the problem at hand. That's something you can achieve through practice. In the meantime, in the following chapter, we'll look at metaheuristics and how they differ from conventional heuristics. Stay tuned!

CHAPTER 3

Heuristics versus Metaheuristics

3.1 Metaheuristics overview

Let's now shift gears and talk about metaheuristics, which are conceptually different from heuristics. A metaheuristic is a high-level problem-independent algorithmic framework that provides a set of guidelines or strategies for developing heuristic optimization algorithms. Often the whole optimization algorithm is referred to as a metaheuristic. Also, it's not unheard of to utilize other, simpler and more general heuristics in it, much like ensemble models makes use of simpler models in the back-end. This same idea is utilized in many data models these days and some advanced optimization methods, as we'll see later on in this book.

Metaheuristics came about because conventional optimization algorithms could not tackle modern problems in data-related fields. Moreover, sometimes even conventional problems solvable with traditional optimizers are better tackled with metaheuristics since the conventional approach would require more time or computational resources. This latter issue made it impossible to solve such problems at scale, which made the development of metaheuristics imperative.

A lesser-known benefit of metaheuristics is that they express a different way of thinking about a problem. Instead of finding the absolute best solution, they involve some randomness and compromises when it comes to the accuracy of this solution. This may seem like heresy to a mathematician, but in practice, an approximate solution is much more preferable than an accurate solution that takes ages to come about. So, in a way, metaheuristics are more aligned with an engineering approach to problem-solving.

We care more about a good enough solution than a mathematically elegant one unreachable in practice.

You can also view metaheuristics as a creative way to handle complex optimization problems. Instead of taking the more established road, you venture on an alternative path, which will be better for the problem at hand. After all, there are no panaceas in problem-solving, at least when it comes to something feasible with our current technology (quantum computing technology is very promising, but it's not there yet). In many scenarios involving such problems, this creativity tool is the best one at our disposal.

In this book, we'll classify metaheuristics as a kind of heuristics. You can view this taxonomy in Figure 3.1 below. In practice, you may find that the various categories depicted in this diagram overlap.

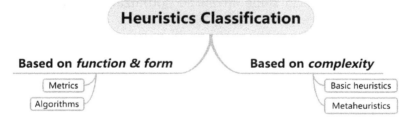

Fig. 3.1 A classification of the various heuristics types. May be overlaps between categories.

3.2 When to use metaheuristics

Metaheuristics are quite popular for tackling complex optimization problems, particularly when many variables are involved. If you have tried solving such a problem with more than a handful of variables, you would know that the complexity grows exponentially with the number of variables. What's more, in several optimization problems, we don't know the derivatives of the objective function involved with those variables (it may even be the case that there are no derivatives). So, conventional optimizers that use derivatives aren't applicable in these cases (since the derivatives data isn't available), making it imperative that we leverage heuristics-based alternatives.

Additionally, finding the objective function's value in many cases is straightforward and doesn't require a high computational cost. Therefore, we can employ a series of such values and use them in tandem. Think of this as a "swarm" of solutions—it's a very popular concept in many metaheuristics. We'll talk more about them later on in this book.

Alternatively, we may not be able to calculate lots of values for the objective function because it takes a lot of time or computational resources to do so. In this case, we may need to be more frugal with how often we call it, so we opt for an optimization strategy that doesn't require many steps. This translates into an entirely different metaheuristic altogether. Of course, this can be a variation of an existing one, so it's always useful to be aware of the various metaheuristics and their application.

Since the space of possibilities related to the different metaheuristics can exist is vast, the sky is the limit when using this kind of creativity tool. However, when employing a new metaheuristic, it may take some time to make sure it works well enough to add value. That's why it's best to save metaheuristics for problems where conventional approaches aren't viable or practical.

Finally, you can use metaheuristics whenever you research new ways to solve optimization problems. However, this doesn't mean that you need to be a professional researcher. For example, you may need to optimize a particular process and aren't satisfied with the performance of other optimizers, so you may decide to tweak one and create your own metaheuristic variant. This metaheuristic may not have universal value, but it may be the best solution for that particular problem.

3.3 Problems lending themselves to metaheuristics

Typical scenarios where metaheuristics come into play are NP-hard problems (see glossary for definition). Specifically, when it comes to data science, many data engineering-related tasks are NP-hard problems. A typical scenario involves feature selection when the original feature set is enormous and you need to consider the correlations among the various features. Of course, you could always take the correlation of each feature to the target variable if you have one, but that won't always yield as robust a solution. You can view this approach as a heuristic of sorts that can be helpful in the case of a proof-of-concept project.

Clustering is another metaheuristic-related problem. This is a classical NP-hard problem, which is challenging to solve. That's one of the reasons why there are so many clustering algorithms out there. It cannot be tackled easily in a deterministic way (though it is possible, with the right heuristics!), making it a problem commonly solved with stochastic algorithms. Clustering uses various kinds of heuristics and metaheuristics (wherever optimization is involved). Note that in the case of clustering, the complexity stems from the number of data points, rather than the number of features (dimensions), and the fact that there are too many potential solutions. Fortunately, since we often use clustering for data exploration, no one is too strict about the exactness of the solution. This makes heuristics and metaheuristics an ideal option for this kind of problem.

Moreover, various kinds of data synthesis involve problems that we can tackle with metaheuristics. Data synthesis is the creation of new data points that follow the same patterns (geometry) of the original dataset. Although this task may seem straightforward for lower dimensionality data, it's quite challenging when many features are involved. It's very easy to create data points using some random function, but to make them aligned with the patterns of the original dataset is an NP-hard problem. Fortunately, with the right heuristics and metaheuristics, this task becomes manageable. We often use an AI system called an autoencoder for this sort of application.

Finally, data summarization, a type of effective data reduction, also lends itself to metaheuristics. This kind of task is akin to sampling but much more sophisticated and precise. Instead of picking data points randomly, the selection occurs more methodically and deterministically. Sometimes, new data points are created, much like in data synthesis, though in this case, they are aggregates of the original data points. To summarize data effectively, you need to use a metaheuristic. Otherwise, the result isn't valuable or takes a very long time to process. The new dataset contains the same patterns as the original one, but it's smaller. Creating such a reduced dataset can offer many advantages, such as conserving computational resources.

There are several other problems that we can solve with metaheuristics, so keep an open mind about metaheuristics and their promising approach to tackling complex problems.

3.4 Important considerations

Although metaheuristics are brilliant, they aren't always plug-and-play or even the best way to go in certain cases. A metaheuristic may yield a good solution but it doesn't usually yield reproducibility of that solution. So, if someone else tries to solve the same problem with the same metaheuristic-powered algorithm, he is bound to arrive at a slightly different solution. This is common among all processes that involve randomness, such as stochastic processes. Since all metaheuristics are in this category, they are unpredictable and unreproducible by nature. Fortunately, there is a way to bypass this issue by using pseudo-random numbers and keeping track of the seed value used for the experiments.

Another thing that's good to keep in mind is that metaheuristics often involve a set of parameters that greatly influence their functionality. So, they aren't super simple to use, and even if the default parameter values are acceptable, they may not yield the desired results. To bypass this issue, you can learn about the metaheuristic's parameters and adjust them properly. When you first use a metaheuristic, you may need to run it a few times with different parameter values to understand how these values affect the results. Furthermore, it's best to first consult the metaheuristic's documentation, if available. Oftentimes, a metaheuristic is the product of some serious research in the optimization field (which falls under AI, by the way). So, if you can look into it, perhaps even at the corresponding papers published on that topic, it would be to your advantage. However, if that's not an option (some of these papers are hard to access), you can resort to a presentation or a tutorial describing that metaheuristic.

Metaheuristics do not work well in some particular scenarios. They may be brilliant, but if they don't solve your problem, explore other options or perhaps come up with your own. Like conventional heuristics, metaheuristics are supposed to help your creativity, not limit it by putting it in a box.

3.5 Summary

We distinguished metaheuristics from heuristics. Heuristics are metrics or methods that help us tackle problems creatively, while metaheuristics solve optimization problems. Due to their nature, metaheuristics are somewhat more sophisticated and specialized, though very useful for complex problems. Additionally, we saw that metaheuristics lend themselves to certain problems under NP-hard, such as feature selection when there are many features, clustering, data synthesis, and data summarization. Note that these problems are data science-specific and that metaheuristics can also tackle various other problems. Finally, we highlighted some important considerations for metaheuristics, like the fact that they have a set of parameters that influence the algorithms' performance.

The next chapter will examine specialized methods and metrics as heuristics. We'll explore how they add value to a data science project, how they manifest in practice, and when to use each one of these kinds of heuristics. So, grab some coffee and see you in a bit!

CHAPTER 4

Specialized Metrics and Methods

4.1 Why heuristics are essential

Although we have a plethora of options for tackling data, be it through models or Extract, Transform, and Load (ETL) tools, heuristics are preferred because of how we work when it comes to complex problems. What's more, this is something unlikely to change in the near future, even if automation is becoming more and more widespread.

Heuristics are scalable and therefore easy to plug into existing algorithms or use them on their own, to get a better perspective of the entire dataset. This is particularly important in the era of big data, where high-performance data tools are no longer nice-to-have but a necessity.

What's more, heuristics are data-driven, so they look at the data as it is, rather than how we'd like it to be to make our lives easier. This objectivity is rare among other metrics, which tend to be biased because of the data's distribution-related assumptions. Heuristics are more akin to machine learning than statistics. That's not to say that statistical metrics have no merit, but rather that they are not part of this new data-driven paradigm of dealing with data, which has been on the rise these past few years. Considering how valuable this approach is to the business world, this trend will continue.

Although they cannot substitute for data models, heuristics are easy to interpret and communicate, and usually do not require knowledge of advanced math.

Finally, heuristics are sometimes the only option for solving a problem.

4.2 How heuristics manifest in practice

But how do heuristics manifest in practice in our data-related work? Through specialized metrics and methods. In addition to other kinds of algorithms, methods can encompass metaheuristics. In any case, how they manifest depends on the problem at hand. That's why it's good to first have a clear idea of what you want out of a heuristic. Because no matter how powerful a heuristic is, it's not practical to use it in the place of a data model. The latter may make use of heuristics in the back-end, but it cannot be easily replaced by a single heuristic.

So, we need to understand what the heuristic needs to achieve and define its scope. Otherwise, it's easy to misuse a heuristic, wasting time and resources. We also need to be clear about the heuristic's functionality and its resource usage. Otherwise, it would be difficult to scale.

It's important to know using a heuristic is work in progress, and therefore we need to manage our expectations accordingly. Still, it's probably better than the alternative, plus if it's not perfect, it means we can always improve it. That may not be easy, but it's usually doable.

Finally, the heuristic is bound to manifest either in an existing form, such as a previously created heuristic or a potential heuristic. In the former case, we just need to use some pre-existing code or code the algorithm involved if we just have access to that.

Usually, it's not that difficult to implement a heuristic programmatically, though it may not be as simple to make it scale well. That's why it's important to understand its scope and functionality before attempting anything. Also, as long as the heuristic can help us solve a problem more efficiently, that should be good enough to get started.

4.3 When to use a specialized metric

Let's now examine how a heuristic can take the form of a metric and when this can be of value to our work. Metric-related heuristics are different than statistical metrics. A statistical metric is backed by theory, a mathematical model, and a set of underlying assumptions. A metric-related heuristics is a simple mathematical object that attempts to express something which can bring value to our problem-solving endeavors.

So, in Exploratory Data Analysis (EDA), for example, we have a bunch of specialized metrics that are used as heuristics to help us understand the data better. There is no shortage of tools to use from the various similarity metrics (e.g., *rank correlation, Jaccard similarity,* and *cosine similarity*), to more sophisticated metrics from information theory (e.g., *entropy* and *mutual information*). More often than not, when we have a particular variable that we need to predict, usually in a Classification or Regression setting, we tend to compare the various features with that variable. This can be the basis of feature selection, for example. We'll talk more about this later.

Moreover, in feature engineering, specialized metrics can add value as heuristics. Although method-related heuristics usually make the most noticeable impact, metrics can also support that. For example, suppose we have a heuristic to measure the relationship between a feature and the target variable accurately. In this case, we can leverage that for assessing new metafeatures that stem from some combination of the existing features (like PCA does but better). As a bonus, you can maintain some transparency in those metafeatures, which can come in handy if you want to backtrack your predictions to its original features. In other words, you can replicate the value-add of PCA, without relying on that method, which although brilliant, doesn't scale all that well.

Additionally, when training a model in the data learning phase, we often employ a heuristic metric, as in a decision tree and any ensembles based on that data model. Depending on what version of the decision tree model you examine, you'll find a key heuristic for figuring out which feature to use next and where to perform the split if there are continuous features. Other machine learning models have a similar "secret sauce" under the hood, as in the case of certain K nearest neighbor variants, which go beyond just the neighborhood by leveraging the geometry of the dataset. For example, the fuzzy knn model uses a similarity heuristic based on distances. Note that today's more advanced models may not employ such obvious heuristic metrics. Still, they may use some heuristic-based training algorithm (e.g., most Artificial Neural Networks) or some specialized data transformation function for creating metafeatures on the fly (mostly ANNs).

Finally, when summarizing the findings of your work in the final stage of the pipeline, we may use a heuristic metric to capture the performance of our model of choice. So, when we need to defend our decision to the project stakeholders, we can rely on something more than just "this model is state-of-the-art" and quote some performance scores. These scores tend to come from specialized heuristics such as the F1 metric, the Area Under Curve, the Mean Squared Error, etc. Note that none of these are stats-related, even if they apply to statistical models too for evaluating their performance.

4.4 When to use a specialized method

What if a heuristic metric isn't enough? We can still leverage method-related heuristics and gain value from them instead. After all, in the original uses of heuristics in mathematical problem-solving, heuristics were more like methods and tactics than anything else. This is particularly the case nowadays in the analytics arena, as most of the problems we encounter are challenging and complex enough to render such a strategy.

For starters, in the EDA phase, we can use method-related heuristics to determine the best features for predicting a certain variable. However, the whole process of selecting a subset of features goes beyond using a similarity metric. A specialized method for selecting these subsets and refining this selection must be in place. Otherwise, the whole feature selection process would be trivial and probably ineffective. For example, we may build the subset from scratch or start with the whole feature-set and gradually make it lighter by removing the most information-poor features. In any case, we would need a heuristic method would to make this happen.

Additionally, in feature engineering, you can rely on the same similarity metrics for evaluating a feature, or rather a metafeature. The latter is something you can put together by creating a custom combination of two or more features, using a set of operators of your choice. PCA does something like this, using the weighted sum, to optimize the metafeatures in terms of variance explained. However, you can use other, more sophisticated ways to fuse features. For example, autoencoders do exactly that, using specialized functions (usually the sigmoid one) for each feature and metafeature, before applying the weighted sum approach. Also, they try to minimize an error heuristic metric between the reconstructed features and the original ones.

Moreover, when training a model in the data learning phase, you also need to employ a specialized method kind of heuristic, especially when dealing with machine learning models. We call this the *training algorithm*. It involves some kind of optimization and some heuristic metric that is maximized or minimized. If the optimization is not present, it's probably because the model opts for simplicity and involves one or more parameters that the user optimizes. These are often referred to as meta-parameters since they are beyond the model itself (at least in the minds of those people who came up with this somewhat confusing term!).

Beyond that, we could use method-related heuristics when researching alternative ways to manage data. For example, we can employ a custom encoding that can enable better compression for a dataset. Moreover, this kind of method can help merge different data structures (e.g., vectors, matrices, or dictionaries) into a single data file, which we can access through the reverse heuristic process. You don't need to implement the compression algorithm from scratch, since there are some pretty good ones already implemented by qualified coders, even in the Julia ecosystem. The above example is one I developed myself a couple of years ago to manage datasets (not just the data in them but also all metadata deriving from it and comments).

Finally, there are optimization-related applications where heuristics, particularly metaheuristics, shine. These specialized methods provide a lot of value in various problems, even beyond the analytics domain. Even if these methods are referred to with a different name, they are still heuristics. In fact, they are closer to the original definition of heuristics used in math.

4.5 Summary

We saw how to leverage specialized metrics and methods as heuristics in various parts of the data science pipeline, extending to other analytics-related work. Since sometimes heuristics are our only option while they are also very efficient and scalable, it's good to know about them and how they add value to our problem-solving endeavors. We saw how to use specialized metrics as heuristics in various scenarios, such as EDA, feature engineering, training data models, and summarizing findings. Furthermore, we explored how we can use specialized methods as heuristics, often in combination with some of the previous heuristic metrics. This is the case for feature selection, model training, data management, and specialized applications like optimization.

In the next chapter, we'll go into more depth on EDA-related heuristics, starting from the most basic ones. Also, you may want to get your computer ready since this chapter will involve some coding. If you haven't prepared your coding environment yet, check out Appendix B.

PART II

Data-oriented Heuristics

This is the essence of intuitive heuristics: when faced with a difficult question, we often answer an easier one instead, usually without noticing the substitution.

Daniel Kahneman

CHAPTER 5

Basic Heuristics for EDA

5.1 EDA heuristics overview

Exploratory Data Analysis (EDA) is a fairly straightforward process, so why would we want to bother with heuristics? Heuristics make the whole process easier, especially when complex data is involved. Instead of going through plots to figure out what's happening in the dataset, you can calculate metrics for the various variables and their relationships, obtaining a comprehensive summary of the dataset. Then, optionally, you can plot that summary and some of the variables that stand out. This way, you can get a head start on your EDA work while doing something that makes you stand out a bit from other data professionals.

Additionally, basic heuristics are easy to implement and use. Combined with the fact that these heuristics can offer you a different angle of the dataset, something that statistics cannot provide. As a bonus, you don't need to give up your other tools for EDA, since heuristics can work in parallel. For example, we often need to choose what models we train in data model building since that's a time-consuming process. With EDA tools, on the other hand, this is not a concern since all of these tools are generally fast.

What's more, basic heuristics can often provide an in-depth view of the dataset. This can bring about valuable insights and steer your data model building in a better direction. Sometimes we forget that most data analytics (and data science to some extent) work is usually in this part of the pipeline. If this can be accelerated or improved through heuristics, that's a good value proposition. This is particularly the case when the dataset is complex enough, and conventional EDA methods fail to yield anything useful, or if they do, they require specialized expertise.

Furthermore, it's usually just unknown variables with unknown relationships when you first start your exploration of the dataset. At this point, it's premature to make any assumptions about the data, while any assumptions you plan to make are bound to weigh on the prep work you do on the dataset at this stage. So, if you want to get a good idea of what's happening in the dataset, it's a no-brainer that basic heuristics are the best strategy. Of course, you can always supplement it with additional EDA tools, like histograms and other plots, but these heuristics can be a good starting point. This is particularly the case if you are familiar with them from other datasets and comfortable using them in a new dataset.

EDA is the most creative part of the pipeline with no rigid rules for its application. In fact, the more tools you use, the better your results.

5.2 Basic heuristics in EDA

Let's now look at basic heuristics that shine when it comes to EDA. Namely, let's look at a non-linear correlation metric and some binary correlation ones. All features can be either continuous or binary after processing them. Of course, there are also ordinal features, but most people in our field choose to treat them as one of the previous two categories due to the lack of specialized metrics. Note that these aren't the only such heuristic metrics available, but they are a good start.

The non-linear correlation metric can be useful when we have two variables with a complex relationship that we need to gauge. For example, suppose we have a continuous feature and a continuous target variable correlated in a non-linear way. We may still need to use that fact since that feature may be useful in a non-linear model. But to know that, we need to measure it, and since the conventional correlation metric tracks linear correlation only, we need to use something else.

Binary correlation metrics are useful when we have many binary features correlated with each other. If that's the case, we may need to eliminate some of them, but we need to measure their correlations to know which ones to remove. We could perform a similar analysis for the relationship between these features and a binary target variable in the case of a binary classification problem.

5.2.1 The range based correlation heuristic

The non-linear correlation heuristic metric mentioned previously is based on ranges, hence its name, *Range Based Correlation* (RBC). This heuristic is based on the product of the author's research on this topic, to analyze these non-linear relationships among features and the target variable, in many regression scenarios. Also, there is something peculiar about this heuristic's logic and overall approach to finding the relationship of the variables analyzed. It's a particular idea that's very popular these days, at least in other domains. However, don't worry if it doesn't come to you, as we'll revisit it in Chapter 16.

RBC uses geometry to gauge if a relationship is non-linear by using the fluctuations of the data points of the two variables analyzed and the worst-case scenario for each data point fluctuation. Since the range of these fluctuations is set, we can use that as a normalizing factor, ensuring that the heuristic takes values between 0 and 1 (inclusive). To avoid additional complications, we use normalized variables here that each have a range of 1. This is a fair assumption to make since more often than not, we deal with normalized variables. In any case, the method works well even if we don't normalize the variables since it does so independently.

Since the RBC metric checks every consecutive pair of data points, it may be misled by the random variations present. That's why it's best to work with a smaller dataset, such as one derived from sampling. Of course, you can always enable sampling through a parameter in the rbc() function provided in the codebook. If you have not yet downloaded the codebook, you can find it at https://technicspub.com/TheDataPathLessTraveled. Sampling can also make the method more scalable and reliable for real-world datasets.

The main idea of the RBC metric lies in its heuristic, namely how it deals with a single pair of consecutive data points, A(x1, y1) and B(x2, y2), where x and y are the two variables whose relationship we explore. We first connect the two data points with a straight line. Then we find the worst-case scenario where we could have gone from point A. This can be either to the top of the scale, point C(x2, 1.0), or to the bottom of it, point D(x2, 0.0). Of course, we could have just continued in some linear fashion to point E(x2, d), where d is the projected value of y if x followed y linearly all along. Using points C, D, and E, we can create the necessary context for the actual change of coordinates, depicted by the length of AB. The context takes the form of two numbers, the minimum possible distance dm and the maximum possible distance dM. Subtracting one from the other yields the range of all possible distances between those two points, rd. Using dm and rd, we can then normalize the actual distance AB to get a number nd between 0.5 and 1.0, inclusive. With some basic linear transformation of that metric, we can turn it into one that takes values between 0.0 and 1.0.

The RBC metric considers all the data point pairs (the various nd values), aggregating them through the median function and applying the aforementioned transformation. A high RBC value (i.e., close to 1.0) denotes a strong relationship while a low value (i.e., close to 0.0) signifies a lack of a relationship. RBC captures everything, including linear relationships, since we made no assumptions about the nature of this relationship between x and y.

5.2.2 Binary correlation heuristics

The binary correlation heuristics we had in mind for this section are a variant of the accuracy rate and another one of the Jaccard similarity (not to be confused with the Jaccard Index, which applies to sets).

Probably you are already quite familiar with the accuracy rate metric for evaluating a binary classifier. However, this has its limitations too, since it's designed for that particular function and is not as useful for general evaluation of the relationship between two binary features. For that purpose, we have the symmetric similarity index (SSI), which generalizes the accuracy rate.

So, say we have a contingency table like this:

Variable 1 | Variable 2	True (1)	False (0)
True (1)	a	b
False (0)	c	d

Let's imagine that variable 2 is the target variable we'd be able to calculate the accuracy rate as follows: AR = (a+d) / (a+b+c+d) = (a+d) / N, where N is the total number of data points. In essence, we take the sum of the main diagonal and divide it by the total.

Clearly, the AR metric takes high values if the two binary variables are aligned. Wouldn't it be as well if they were completely misaligned though? Imagine that each data point represents two people expressing a state or opinion on a yes-no matter (e.g., a building located in the Western or the Eastern hemisphere, a fan being for this or the other soccer team in the upcoming match, etc.). Each person is one of the variables in this example, and the various topics are the data points. Obviously, if the two people agree on everything, having both of them present in a meeting is redundant. We immediately know what the other person will say if we hear the first person. Also, it's not too difficult to see that if the two people disagreed on more or less everything, we'd have a similar situation. In this case, we'd just have to reverse the view of person A to know the view of person B, on any given matter. So, even if the two variables are misaligned, they can still be strongly correlated, even if AR would take a value of 0.0 in that case. How can we express all that with a heuristic metric?

Well, we can use the other diagonal of the confusion matrix too. So, if x_0 is the AR based on that matrix, we can also compute x_1 by taking the complementary AR, namely $(b + c) / N$. Then we can select the largest of the two and use that value (i.e., $\max(x_0, x_1)$). This value, however, is bound to be between 0.5 and 1.0, so if we want our metric to be between 0.0 and 1.0, we'll need to apply a linear transformation. This new metric, which I refer to as Symmetric Similarity Index (SSI), yields high values if the variables x and y are somehow similar, even if one is the reverse of the other. SSI yields low value when x and y are not related at all. That is, they cover all possibilities of true and false equally likely.

Let's now look at the Jaccard similarity metric, a useful heuristic that focuses on one particular value of the binary variable (usually the value true, also known as 1), so the relationship between the binary variables is mainly based on that value. This is very useful for evaluating the outputs of binary classifiers, though we can use it for features too. Using the confusion matrix we looked at previously, Jaccard similarity is defined as $a / (a + b + c)$ and takes values between 0 and 1. Although this can be useful in the aforementioned binary classification scenario, it's biased in everything else. Enter the Symmetric Jaccard Similarity heuristic.

Symmetric Jaccard Similarity, or SJS, aims to balance this biased metric by leveraging its symmetrical counterpart. If two features are very similar, even if we reverse their polarities like in the previous example, they should still score high in this metric. Of course, Jaccard Similarity focuses on a particular value (the value *true*), so the symmetric Jaccard similarity follows the same pattern. That's not bad necessarily, since in many applications in Analytics, one value is more important to us than the other (e.g., in the case of a customer buying a product). SJS captures that by taking the maximum of the two Jaccard similarities: the original one (J1) and the one with one of the variables reversed (J2 = d / (b + c + d)). Also, just like the original Jaccard similarity, SJS takes values between 0.0 and 1.0, inclusive, with higher values denoting a stronger relationship between the two variables.

5.2.3 Your own heuristics

Beyond these heuristic metrics, several similar ones are available. For example, you can look into ways to generalize the binary correlation metrics applied to nominal variables. Alternatively, you can look into ways to gauge the relationship between two ordinal variables, though that may take a different kind of heuristic to work well. There is plenty of room for heuristics development, and EDA is a broad area with great potential for value-adds. The sandbox section in the codebook of this chapter could be a good place for you to experiment with this.

5.3 How you can leverage these heuristics in EDA effectively

But how is it best to efficiently and effectively apply these heuristics for EDA work? Well, you first need to identify scenarios where they can add value. For example, there is no point in applying them in variables where the relationship is obvious since you have already plotted them and a clear pattern emerged. Clearly, the most fundamental aspect of the variables you examine is their type. If the types match (both variables are continuous or both variables are binary), you can apply one of the most relevant heuristic metrics from those we examined.

These heuristics yield some useful information about the variables' alignment. So, if you have processes in place that involve this kind of information, you can use them in tandem with these heuristics. A typical scenario is feature selection, where you need to filter the variables in place based on how well they correlate with the target variable. When you have many variables in your dataset, this process is often essential and can save you a lot of time. Another relevant process is feature fusion, where you combine different features to develop new ones (metafeatures) that are better at predicting the target variable. You can optimize these metafeatures using the heuristics above and any other necessary factors.

An automated or semi-automated process is the most efficient use of these heuristics and any other heuristics of the same category. After all, it would be masochistic to apply them to each pair of variables in the dataset manually, especially when there are lots of features involved. So, creating a Julia script that leverages these heuristics is a good option. This script can identify all the continuous variables, for example, and apply RBC to them, while it can do the same for all the binary variables it finds. How you develop this script would depend on the function you need it to perform and the type of target variable you have.

It's important to note that we can tweak heuristics if they don't work properly for our problem. For example, when assessing the relationship of two binary variables and in your problem, one of the two states of the binary variables is more important, you can assign weights to the SJS metric. Naturally, you are better off documenting your work and adding some comments to the script you are using to avoid any future issues with that heuristic.

5.4 Important considerations

Before we close this chapter, there are some important considerations to avoid misuse. For instance, it would be a big problem if you used any one of these heuristics for the wrong type of variable. Just because a variable is expressed numerically (as a number), it doesn't mean it is numeric (continuous). That's why it's best to look into it in more depth, analyzing its value structure. Perhaps it's a binary variable in disguise or even a categorical one. So, make extra sure that the variables are what they are supposed to be before you input them into the functions of the heuristic metrics.

What's more, these metrics are by no means a substitute for diligent analytics work, particularly in the EDA stage. They can add a lot of value, but you can't rely on them exclusively. A plot may yield a lot of insight, perhaps more than any metric could, at least in some cases. So, it's best to use these metrics with other EDA tools for optimal results. Otherwise, you may miss some significant insights, hindering your progress in the project.

Also, realize that these heuristics, particularly those related to the binary variables, are not always suitable for the problem. If, for example, the dataset is heavily biased towards one or the other value in these variables, the metrics may not yield a valuable result. This is particularly the case when one of these variables is the target variable (classification problem), and the whole dataset is therefore biased. Sometimes, you need to preprocess the dataset to ensure that the classes are balanced. This can save you a lot of work in the later stages of the pipeline.

Finally, the RBC heuristic employs some (deterministic) sampling as an option (i.e., the smoothing parameter *sf* is greater than 1). If this happens, the value it yields is bound to change (not drastically, but measurably for sure). If you have many data points, you can still evaluate the variables without spending too much time. However, you need to keep in mind the parameter value used if you compare the RBC values of various pairs of variables. Otherwise, the metric may lead you to wrong conclusions about the dataset examined.

5.5 Summary

We explored some basic heuristics and how to leverage them in the EDA part of the pipeline. Specifically, we saw that basic heuristics are a great value-add for EDA because they offer a different and often better perspective, all while not compromising on your other tools. We looked at a few specific basic heuristics that are great for EDA and require minimal prep work. Metrics like RBC are ideal for continuous variables, while SSI and SJS are great when binary variables are at play. RBC can handle all kinds of relationships between continuous variables, including non-linear ones. SSI and SJS, can evaluate similarities even if the binary variables have an inverse relationship. We explored ways to effectively leverage these heuristics in EDA, such as in feature selection and feature fusion applications. Also, they are better off being part of an automated or semi-automated process, especially if many variables are involved in the dataset. Finally, we covered some important considerations, such as ensuring we use the right kinds of variables.

Now would be a great time to look at the Neptune notebook corresponding to this chapter to learn more about this topic. If you have not yet downloaded the notebook, you can find it at https://technicspub.com/TheDataPathLessTraveled. Then, when you are comfortable with this new material, feel free to proceed to the next chapter, where we'll look at some more advanced heuristics for EDA work.

CHAPTER 6

Advanced Heuristics for EDA

6.1 The whys of advanced heuristics in EDA

So far, we have seen some basic heuristics to help us explore a dataset and evaluate certain variable pairs. That's great, but what about going deeper into the data and getting acquainted with its geometry? Unfortunately, the heuristics we've seen so far can't help us with this. However, some advanced heuristics can provide us with much insight into this matter. In addition, these heuristics can complement the other ones we've examined, so it's not an "either-or" kind of situation. Furthermore, the different tools we learn and master tend to build on each other rather than compete.

Advanced heuristics in EDA is a broad field overall. Someone could do a whole research project thesis in this area—and that's something I did during my PhD for one of the heuristics in this chapter. After all, everything in the data science world is interconnected, especially when it comes to the data-driven aspects of the field. So, if you were to go deep into advanced heuristics, you would encounter various aspects of the field and gain a deeper understanding of how data science works.

Therefore, advanced heuristics are excellent creativity tools. They can help analyze the data creatively, eluding many conventional approaches such as plots. Plots are great for getting an overview of the data and understanding the distributions involved. However, this comes at a cost, namely their inability to go into detail or express certain properties of the dataset with precision. As a result, we need something else to go deep into the data and be able to perform more complex transformations that can aid our creativity in tackling the problems involved. After all, the deeper we can go into the data, the more options we'll have to transform it in meaningful ways and build models that express its signals.

It's easy to get into the habit of analyzing specific variables or pairs of variables using similarity metrics, like the basic heuristics we examined previously. However, this sort of analysis can only help us so much. The more variables we have, the richer the dataset, especially with low correlation. However, this marginal benefit of a new variable tends to decrease as the data increases. That's one of the big data challenges and one of the problems data science is tasked with, especially in projects today. That's why it's paramount to be able to examine the dataset in various ways, including some that go into its geometry as a whole, rather than look at its various two-dimensional facets. Just like it's hard to understand a shape by looking at just its shadow, it's difficult to understand a dataset by looking at just pairs of variables. However, certain types of advanced heuristics excel at these problems.

This chapter will look at a couple of advanced heuristics applicable in EDA work. Namely, we'll look at the Index of Discernibility and a couple of Density metrics. Next, we'll explore how you can leverage these heuristics effectively when exploring a dataset. Finally, we'll continue with some important considerations about these heuristics.

6.2 Specific advanced heuristics in EDA

Let's begin our exploration of this topic of advanced heuristics by looking at a couple of such heuristics, namely the index of discernibility and the density metrics. Refer to the code notebook accompanying this chapter since this is a very hands-on topic. If you have not yet downloaded the notebook, you can find it at https://technicspub.com/TheDataPathLessTraveled.

6.2.1 Index of discernibility

The index of discernibility is a concept expressed in various metrics. Still, we'll limit our exploration of it to just one of them—one of the most powerful heuristics for EDA classification projects. It's seen several variations over the years. We will focus on a lighter version of the original metric, which is significantly faster due to some filtering of the data points in the dataset.

In any case, the index of discernibility is a heuristic designed to tell us two things: how discernible any given data point of the dataset is in relation to the classes of that dataset, and how discernible the whole dataset is. In other words, if we are given a data point in that dataset, how easy would it be to tell whether it belongs to its proper class or some other class? Although this sounds like a classifier, it is not. The heuristic doesn't try to classify anything; it just looks at the geometry of the dataset and figures out how well each data point fits into its class. The higher the discernibility, the easier the classification afterwards, regardless of what classifier we use.

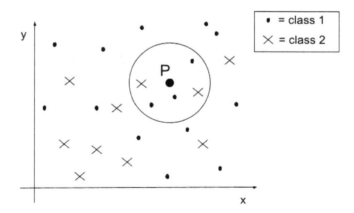

Fig. 6.1 Calculating the index of discernibility for a given point P. Since P is of the first class and there are three other points of that class in the neighborhood and only two points of the second class, the ID of P is equal to (3+1)/(4 + 2) = 0.667 approximately. This is a marginally good score since it's closer to 1 than 0.

The index of discernibility works by using hyperspheres around each data point P (see Figure 6.1). There are bound to be some data points around our data point of choice in each hypersphere. By doing some basic math to find the proportion of the data points of the same class as point P, we calculate the index of discernibility of that data point. Then, by aggregating all the discernibility values across all data points using the median metric, we calculate the index of discernibility of the whole dataset. Naturally, this heuristic takes values between 0 and 1, inclusive, and higher values are generally better. As a rule of thumb, any value over 0.5 is considered good.

Note that the index of discernibility can also be applied to individual features by using each of them instead of the dataset and handling each data point as a one-dimensional point. This can provide us with useful insights into how powerful the individual features are as predictors of the target variable. Note that the distributions of these features are not taken into account. Clearly, that same idea that we saw in RBC (and which we'll see again later in this book) comes into play.

6.2.2 Density analysis

Although we use density in statistics (probability density), it's a different yet powerful metric in data-driven analytics. Furthermore, it's quite straightforward to understand as it's based on an idea from physics that most people are already familiar with, even if it's underrated in that field as there are other, more useful metrics in a physicist's toolkit.

Density involves how crowded a particular part of the data space is. We can evaluate this either around a random point or around a point that belongs to the dataset itself. In both cases, the process is the same, though when you focus on existing data points in the data at hand, it's extra useful as it lets you get an idea of how dense the dataset is overall. After all, what's simpler than taking the number of data points within a given space and dividing it by the volume of that space?

The key issue with density, which everyone seems to avoid addressing, is that unlike the index of discernibility, which works with specific data points within a given area, density works with data points *and* volumes of space (hyper-volumes of hyper-space in many cases). Even if it's relatively easy to draw some hypersphere around a given data point and find the points that dwell within, doing so for density would be highly problematic. This is because of the highly irregular behavior of the volume of hyperspheres when dimensionality increases. So, it would make much more sense to use some other shape, such as a hypercube or some hyper-rectangle, so that calculating its volume (and of density as a result) won't create too much confusion.

So, let's leave the complexities of the hyper-space aside for a while and look at density in the simple, one-dimensional case. In this scenario, we just look at the line of the variable at hand and create a segment around each data point. The length of that segment is usually given by some other heuristic, such as the average distance between two data points multiplied by a constant. Alternatively, we can use the optimal bin length given by the Freedman-Diaconis rule (often applied for finding the optimal number of bins in a histogram). The latter is a more elegant solution and doesn't require assumptions about the length provided. That is, there is no multiplier constant like in the previous strategy.

Having set the length of the segment, we can take half of that length for one side of the data point (e.g., the left side where points with lower values reside) and half of that length for the other side. It's not too difficult to find which points reside in that area and count them. Then we can divide this number by the length of the line segment and we'll have the density of that data point as a result. We can then repeat the same process for the remaining data points. To get an idea of the density of the whole dataset, we can aggregate these density values using an averaging operator such as the median since these densities are bound to be all over the place with outliers reigning supreme.

Now that we have an intuition about how density works in the simple scenario of a single dimension, let's see how it works in more complex dimensionalities. We'll just apply the same process in this scenario but use multiple line segments, one for each dimension. Combining these into a single shape yields a hypercube (a multidimensional cube) that contains many data points and has the given data point in its center. To calculate the density in this case, we apply the same process (counting data points and dividing). Still, instead of dividing by a length we divide by the volume of that hypercube (the length of its side raised to the power of the dataset's dimensionality). Then, to find the overall density of the dataset, we take the average (median) of all the densities of the individual data points.

6.2.3 Other advanced heuristics

Beyond these two heuristics, there are other similar ones based on the same concepts. For example, a new one that I came up with recently involves how peculiar a given data point is. Although it could be, this data point doesn't have to be part of the original dataset. It's called the Index of Peculiarity and is based on a similar geometrical approach to EDA, and can provide various insights about the dataset and the specific data point itself. We'll take a closer look at the index of peculiarity heuristic in Chapter 16, where we'll attempt to build it from scratch.

All this helps illustrate that the whole area of EDA work has a lot of potential for new heuristics of this kind. Also, nothing is set in stone since new and better ones can come about without dedicating a lot of time to that effort. The index of peculiarity heuristic, for example, took about a day from inception to unit testing and creating a Julia script around it, utilized in a specific use case. The idea behind the heuristic is often the hardest part since there aren't that many original ideas out there. However, with enough curiosity and understanding of the data science field, it's possible to develop equally good advanced heuristics, if not better ones, to facilitate your EDA work.

6.3 How to leverage these heuristics in EDA effectively

But how can we put all this into practice and make the most of these advanced heuristics in a data science project? You can turn all your non-continuous variables into binary and normalize all the continuous ones. This is particularly useful for most data science projects anyway, even if you plan to use some AI-based model afterward. Also, it's essential if you want to perform clustering to the dataset as part of the EDA process.

Following this, you can evaluate the densities of the various data points and then the dataset itself by applying an average metric to them, such as the median. If the dataset is of low dimensionality, you can create a plot based on that data, such as a heat map. If there is a target variable present, you can even plot the density in relation to it. In some cases, the density variable can be used as a feature if there exists an interesting correlation between the density of the data points and the target variable—something you can evaluate in various ways, including the RBC heuristic. Note, however, that if you plan to use density this way, you may want to normalize it too, so that it's of the same scale as the other features.

Additionally, you can perform clustering if you find groups of high density in the dataset. Considering that this is often the very definition of a cluster, it's intriguing that most clustering methods don't take density into account. The insights you can derive from exploring the data using density can give you an idea of how many groups to look for. Alternatively, you can let the clustering algorithm decide that, particularly if it's one of the more advanced such algorithms. Note that you may need to do some dimensionality reduction before clustering. It would be interesting to examine if and how the density changes after you do that.

If your dataset includes a target variable, you can use the index of discernibility too. Although this is designed for cases when the target variable is discrete, you can also use it for a continuous target variable if you first make it discrete. You can do the latter using binning (the first step to creating a histogram) or by manually grouping its values into meaningful groups aligned with domain knowledge about that variable, such as high monthly sales values are anything above $100,000. If the dataset doesn't contain a target variable, you can use the cluster labels from your clustering process (this approach could be viewed as a heuristic of sorts too). This will yield relatively high discernibility scores, but it can also be insightful. For example, if these scores are all close to 1.0, it can be interpreted as a very crisp clustering result. Then you can compare these with the average Silhouette Score of the clusters and draw further insights.

Afterward, you can use the index of discernibility to understand the classes of the dataset and how challenging the classification task will be. Perhaps this can determine what kind of method to use for it, or whether it's worth going with an ensemble of classifiers right from the start. The chances are that the dataset is still unrefined at this point in the pipeline, so its discernibility scores will be relatively low. So, it would make sense to repeat this process after you have performed some cleaning and transformations. This can also help you evaluate the effectiveness of the processes involved in the data engineering stage.

Alternatively, you can use this heuristic to evaluate the various features involved and use the insights deriving from this to guide your data engineering tasks. For example, suppose you were to focus on particular data points instead. In that case, you can use the discernibility values of these points to examine if some of them are problematic or not (perhaps they are inliers that you would want to remove or handle somehow). Maybe you can even plot those areas and take a closer look at them. In any case, using the heuristic this way can help you better understand the dataset's challenges and deal with the dataset more effectively.

Beyond these ideas, you can think of some of your own. Remember, these heuristics have many uses so you can experiment with them in different ways. As long as they add value to your work, it's worth spending some time with them. At the very least, they will help you better understand the geometry of the dataset and its more challenging hot spots.

6.4 Important considerations

All this is great, but it may sound too good to be true. After all, just like in every tool in data science, there are precautions for it and things to keep in mind when using it. For example, in the index of discernibility heuristic, we can use a different distance metric to accommodate the more complex datasets involving lots of variables. Using a different distance metric can clearly change the heuristic's outputs, so it's important to decide on that before using it in many different scenarios that you wish to compare afterward. In addition, this distance metric matter is an important factor in every other geometrical heuristic out there (including the index of peculiarity). Tweaking the distance metric can also help you deal with problematic dimensionalities, where the conventional distance metric (Euclidean distance) fails to work properly, as it often happens when the dimensionality of the data is high.

Additionally, just like basic heuristics, these are very hands-on and are better understood through practice. Getting a grip of the ideas behind them is great, and seeing specific examples of their functionality through diagrams is a big plus. However, you can only understand them properly after using them a bit, especially if you apply them to a dataset with meaningful signals. That's why it's important to pay close attention to the Neptune codebook that accompanies this chapter and try to experiment with these heuristics on your own in the sandbox section of that codebook.

Moreover, it's important to remember that just like other heuristics, these ones too can be used in more sophisticated scripts carrying out more complex tasks. The index of discernibility, for example, has been used successfully in various dimensionality reduction applications as well as some classifiers. Some people use a variation of the density heuristic in a clustering algorithm called DBSCAN, although its implementation isn't as easy to comprehend as the heuristic itself. So, when you look at a heuristic like this, it's good to look beyond the bare-bones implementation you come across since the real value of these tools lies in how you use them as part of a bigger system or process.

Furthermore, geometry-based heuristics may not always work that well in higher dimensionalities. The reason is that the distance metrics commonly used in the real world may not always apply when the number of dimensions is very high. Not to worry, however. You can always perform some dimensionality reduction first before applying these heuristics, or you can apply them on individual variables only. Since the whole process of EDA is relatively creative, feel free to use your creativity in how you apply these heuristics. Perhaps you can even develop a new process based on them that scales well in high-dimensionality space.

Finally, it's important to remember the scope of these heuristics. Both of the heuristics we saw in this chapter, for example, apply to continuous variables, though the index of discernibility works with binary variables too. Trying to use these heuristics with ordinal variables, for example, may yield misleading results. The same goes when using them on categorical variables encoded as numbers. It goes without saying that for any heuristic like these, based on geometry in one way or another, you need to normalize the variables first so they are of the same scale. A basic normalization to the interval [0, 1] is fine for this purpose.

6.5 Summary

We examined advanced heuristics for EDA work, focusing on the index of discernibility and density metrics. We saw that they are invaluable when it comes to going deeper into the data and gaining a better understanding of the underlying geometry of a dataset. The index of discernibility metric involves evaluating how discernible the classes of a dataset are (for when the target variable is discrete). It applies both to a data point of the dataset or the dataset as a whole. The index of discernibility could also be applied to individual features to assess their predictive potential. This heuristic makes use of Euclidean distances or any other distance metric.

Density metrics measure how dense different parts of the dataset are and how dense the dataset is overall. Density can be calculated in various ways, though the best one in terms of scalability involves (hyper)cubes, since it's easier to calculate their volume, an essential part of the whole density calculation. In any case, by averaging all the densities of the individual data points, we can obtain the overall density of the dataset.

You can leverage these two heuristics by using them for EDA work, particularly when dealing with complex datasets. When a discrete target variable is present, the index of discernibility can help you evaluate the difficulty of the problem and even figure out which are your strongest features. The density metric can help you in all sorts of problems, particularly when looking for outliers, inliers, and any kind of problematic area in the dataset where predictions tend to be more challenging.

It's important to be mindful of the scope of the heuristics when using them, so that you don't apply them to data that's not suitable as inputs. Additionally, you need to be aware that higher dimensionalities may cause issues for such heuristics that employ distances. Sometimes, tweaking the distance metric can help mitigate this problem.

Now would be a great time to look at the Neptune notebook corresponding to this chapter so that you can get into more depth on these advanced heuristics. Then, feel free to proceed to the next chapter where we'll look at a few heuristics for model-related tasks when you are ready.

CHAPTER 7

Model-related Heuristics

7.1 Overview of model-related heuristics

Model-related heuristics contain metadata of the model to evaluate its effectiveness and other interesting aspects of its performance. As a result, they can shed light on how good the model is and even the reliability of its predictions on a point-by-point basis. This is particularly important for machine learning models, many of which are relatively opaque. For example, the statistical model often yields a probability score for each prediction, but machine learning ones rarely do so (except for ANNs).

Also, conventional metrics like error rate often fail to capture the effectiveness of a model, be it a machine learning or a statistical one. They give us some general idea, but it's often insufficient for understanding it enough to refine it effectively. Certain heuristics add a lot of value in the evaluation part of a model, which is often a crucial stage of the data science pipeline. After all, without a proper evaluation of a model, it's hard to trust and use it effectively, especially when it comes time to deploy and give it unknown data to process. This issue worsens once we deploy the model and issues like data drift come into play.

This chapter will examine a few key heuristics for evaluating and augmenting a model's outputs. We'll look at F scores (particularly the F1 heuristic metric), the RBC heuristic again, the Area Under Curve heuristic metric, and the confidence index. We'll also look at how you can effectively leverage these heuristics in models and how the confidence index metric can help you make some models more transparent. Finally, we'll also talk about some important considerations regarding these heuristics so that you make the most of them without having issues due to their inherent limitations.

This chapter is accompanied by a codebook, which you may want to study to understand better the heuristics and perhaps look into developing variations of them. You can check the glossary at the end of the book for clarifications on certain terms.

7.2 Specific model-related heuristics

7.2.1 F-scores heuristic

F-scores (aka Fβ-scores) are essentially a family of metrics based on a heuristic for evaluating the performance of a classification model. The simplest one is the F1-score which is common in data science and defined as:

$$F_1 = \frac{2 \times P \times R}{P + R}$$

Where P and R are the Precision and Recall of that classifier. If you are familiar with metrics of averaging, notice that F1 is the harmonic mean of precision and recall—a value that lies between the values of P and R but closer to the smaller of the two. So, in a way, the F1 score combines the two metrics, making optimizing this heuristic a worthwhile endeavor. Naturally, we'd want to make this as large as possible since this aligns with better performance in the classification model.

In the more general case, we can parameterize how much each of these two metrics contributes to the score by adding the quantity β, which usually takes various positive values, not always integer ones. The metric is then referred to as Fβ-score and is defined as:

$$F_\beta = \frac{(1+\beta^2) \times P \times R}{\beta^2 \times P + R}$$

Where β takes the value of 1 Fβ and becomes the F1 from before. Also, if β is less than 1 (say 0.5), the metric takes a value closer to the precision metric. So if β is larger than 1 (say 2), Fβ becomes closer to the recall value. Naturally, for any value of β, the Fβ-score is always within 0 and 1 (inclusive), with most values being over 0.5. Just like with the F1-score, higher values are better.

Fβ-score is very useful when we care more about mitigating false positives rather than false negatives or vice-versa. For example, in cases where the dataset is unbalanced in terms of the classes present, this is very useful as it allows us to consider that imbalance in the classifier's evaluation. Note that if you play with the formula a bit, you can express this metric as a function of the confusion matrix's true positives and true negatives involving the classifier's predictions and the target variable. This way, you can go deeper into the heuristic and understand it better, making it more applicable to solving problems.

Note that we define the Fβ-score heuristic for each class so that it can work with multi-class problems too. If that's the case, we may need to calculate several Fβ-scores (one for each class) and take their average.

7.2.2 Area Under Curve heuristic

The Area Under Curve (AUC) heuristic is another metric for evaluating the performance of classification models, particularly those involving two classes. This is part of the Receiver Operating Characteristics (ROC) analysis and involves a performance curve depicting the relationship between False Positive Rate (the proportion of false positives in the sample) and True Positive Rate (the proportion of true positives in the sample, also known as Recall). If you are unfamiliar with this sort of evaluation process, Figure 7.1 may be helpful to you.

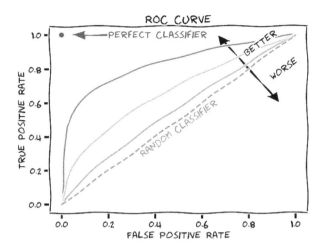

Fig. 7.1 ROC analysis and ROC curves for various classifiers. Source: *sefiks.com*

In practice, the curves in the ROC analysis chart are more like zig-zags, but the more threshold values you use, the smoother the curve seems. The threshold values in ROC analysis involve the different points in the output value beyond which the classifier labels the result as class 1 instead of class 0. ROC works for binary classification, hence the presence of two classes only.

As for the AUC heuristic, this is the area under the curve. Because of the nature of the data in that chart, this area is always between 0 and 1. Usually, we see values higher than 0.5 (which corresponds to the random classifier). Naturally, the higher the value of AUC, the better the classifier's performance.

ROC analysis and the AUC heuristic give us more intuitive insight into the trade-off between false positives and true positives. Also, they help us see which classification model (or version of that model) performs better without getting lost in the details of the various threshold possibilities. Naturally, such a graphic can be very useful in the project's final report.

If we dig deeper into the ROC curve, it could also help us pick the threshold value that seems more appropriate for the problem. To make this decision consider other evaluation metrics involving misclassification costs. We'll discuss one of them in section 7.2.5. There are (at least) a couple of packages in Julia that aim to help with the ROC analysis and the AUC heuristic. Although they both do a lot of the work, it's best to focus on the ROC.jl one since it's much easier to use and more aligned with other packages.

7.2.3 Range based correlation heuristic

Although we've already seen the range based correlation (RBC) heuristic and its usefulness in EDA work, it's worth mentioning here again, as a performance evaluation tool, particularly for regression models. Although there are other, more well-known metrics for regression predictions (such as the mean squared error metric), they tend to be more linear. On the other hand, RBC can capture non-linear relationships between the regressor's outputs and the target variable.

So, even if it doesn't help much to optimize this metric for the model at hand, it can give us a good idea of how close we are to finding a worthwhile regression model. After all, a non-linear relationship between the regressor's predictions with the target variable is better than no relationship at all. So, if we were to use RBC in conjunction with other evaluation metrics, we can gradually refine our regression model and make it provide a more useful output.

7.2.4 Confidence index heuristic

The confidence index heuristic is different from the others discussed because it doesn't work with the model's outputs per se, but rather with the values preceding the outputs. The idea is to measure how sure the model is for each of its predictions on a scale of 0.5 to 1 (inclusive). After all, this can be a level of transparency that can prove invaluable for the end user since it can give him an idea of how likely it is for the prediction to be valid. However, the confidence index is *not* a probability, though we could use a probability as a confidence metric, as in the case of a probabilistic model.

The confidence index takes as inputs the data used by the model to make the prediction right before it calculates the final output. So, in the simple case of a k-nearest neighbor classifier, this data is essentially the neighbors for a given test point. For example, we have n1 points of the winning class and n2 points of all the other classes (n1 > n2 and n1 + n2 = k). The confidence index in this case would be CI = n1 / (n1 + n2) = n1 / k. This makes intuitive sense since if all the points in the neighborhood of that test point are of a particular class (i.e., n1 = k), the confidence of that prediction would be 1.0, which is what we would expect. Because of the nature of this scenario, the confidence index will always be more or equal to 0.5 (if n1 < k/2, it wouldn't be the winning class).

In regression, the confidence index works similarly, but the target variable needs to be analyzed so that we know what kind of values it can take. If it's normalized, the whole matter becomes somewhat easier.

Note that the confidence index is quite subjective, and it's not to be used as a reliability metric. However, in classification, if we were to combine these values with the evaluated outputs vector (i.e., a binary vector containing which predictions were correct and which weren't), we can derive an interesting metric. That metric incorporates both confidence and actual correctness of the outputs and, therefore, can be used as a reliability metric.

7.2.5 Other model heuristics

There are other model-related heuristics in addition to the ones discussed. For example, the misclassification cost heuristic. This heuristic, which applies to various classifiers, involves a cost value, sometimes in a particular currency, for all the misclassifications involved. In a binary classification setting, a misclassification is either a false positive or a false negative.

For example, let's say we have an attrition prediction system to see if a company's customers are bound to leave and take their business to another company. We may decide to approach such customers with a special offer so that they have more reason to stay with our company. In the classifier involved in this project, a false positive would be a person we think will leave but isn't planning to (at least according to the data at hand). A false negative would be a person who we think is happy with the company's services but will leave. Each misclassification is bad for us, but certain misclassifications (like the false negative ones) are worse. So, if a false positive costs us $100 in lost revenue (because of the special offer we give them) and a false negative costs us $1000 (because of the future business of that customer that we won't have any more), the overall cost of our model would be OC = 100*FP + 1000*FN (in dollars). In this scenario, we'd probably want to focus more on mitigating the false negatives of the classifier (improving its precision), since that would help bring down the overall cost more.

So, we can fine-tune our model to minimize that cost OC, instead of maximizing its F1-score, for example. This way, we end up losing less money, even if the overall accuracy of the classifier isn't optimal. We can optimize this by tweaking the decision threshold of our classifier, for example, or choosing a different classification model altogether. This may make some data professionals uncomfortable, so it's good to remember that results matter more than mathematical elegance and precision in the real world.

7.3 How to leverage these heuristics effectively

After a model has yielded its outputs, you can use one of these heuristics to evaluate its performance based on the problem you are tackling. For example, if there is a classification problem, you may want to focus on the Fβ-score and the AUC ones, focusing on the former if there is a class imbalance.

If the model is not very transparent and you need to add some transparency to its function, you can add the confidence index to its outputs. This is particularly easy when dealing with classification scenarios, though it could also work with the right adjustments for regression problems. In any case, having very high or very low values of confidence in the model are a red flag, though higher values may not be as bad if the model's overall performance is high. If a conference speaker seems extra courageous and makes bold assertions, it's not necessarily bad if he's right.

Speaking of regression problems, that's where the RBC heuristic could come in handy for evaluating the model's outputs. Since it's more prone to higher values, it's best to consider that when viewing its value. In addition, it's best if this is used as one of the performance metrics of the regressor so that you can then refine the model. Ideally, you would want a linear relationship with the target variable, but knowing that there is a non-linear relationship may help you work with it better, harnessing that signal.

You can also explore other model-related heuristics, such as a custom cost function for a classification model's false positives and negatives. Although this may seem equivalent to the Fβ-score heuristic, it can be easier to explain and tweak, customizing to the problem. Also, in some cases, its value can be expressed in a monetary value (the total cost of all the misclassifications), making it a useful KPI tool that can be more meaningful to the project stakeholders.

Model-related heuristics are still few and with lots of potential. So, if you find yourself interested in developing new heuristics to facilitate your work and handle this part of the pipeline more creatively, that's something worth exploring. After all, evaluating a model's performance is akin to figuring out how two variables are related, which is a more general problem that lends itself to heuristic-based solutions.

7.4 Important considerations

Just like other heuristics, model-related ones have their peculiarities that we need to be aware of to make the most of them while avoiding falling into any pitfalls related to their function. For example, most of these heuristics can give us an overview of the model's effectiveness, without being able to pinpoint particular issues with its generalization. They may give us valuable insights about how it works with certain predictions, particularly in classification problems, but not for predictions related to individual data points.

The confidence index heuristic addresses this issue to a large extent. Still, it's not as powerful as the other ones since it relies exclusively on inputs from the model. That is, it does not consider the ground truth data. Nevertheless, it may provide some insights into how the model "feels" about the various predictions, which could be helpful, particularly when combined with other information about the model's inner workings. For example, suppose we know that the model works with distances. Then, as in the case of the nearest neighbor family of models, the confidence index may help us troubleshoot the problem of poor performance in certain areas of the dataset, where the data is relatively sparse.

Sometimes, it makes good sense to develop your own heuristics for evaluating a model. Tailor these to the specific characteristics of the problem. Such a heuristic would be able to capture more of what we are interested in regarding the model's performance and help us customize the model to the problem at hand in a more refined way. As a bonus, it's not too difficult to build such a heuristic, at least for classification scenarios.

Additionally, model-related heuristics are as good as the data they work with, just like any other data-driven algorithm. Suppose the sample of the model is biased and the model yields a particular performance (based on these heuristics). In that case, this may not generalize to other data where those biases aren't present. So, heuristics can only help us so much and are in no way a substitute for problematic data, due to bad sampling, for example. Like in other aspects of the pipeline, they have a supporting role here.

Finally, to make the most of these heuristics, it's best to combine them with a K-fold cross-validation process for iterative training and testing of the model. This way, the effect of the biases is mitigated and the model is evaluated more holistically. In that sense, the K-fold cross validation process is a very powerful metaheuristic. When time is limited, you may still be able to manage with a few random overlapping samples, though that may not be as reliable an approach. Large variances among the values of the heuristics are a valuable signal when it comes to that.

7.5 Summary

We looked at various model-related heuristics and how they can help us gauge a model's effectiveness and even augment them to better understand their outputs. We examined the Fβ-score heuristic, an average of the Precision and Recall metrics, related to a classification problem. We also looked at the area under curve (AUC) heuristic as part of the ROC analysis of a binary classifier. This heuristic is very simple to calculate and explain to others. At the same time, it carries a lot of useful information about the classifier and prompts us to tweak its decision parameter to optimize the Recall, if needed. Additionally, we examined the confidence index heuristic, which is a useful tool for transparency in a model, when it's of the opaque kind. Unlike other model-related heuristics, the confidence index doesn't rely on the model's final outputs. Moreover, we explored an alternative model-related heuristic that's quite popular for classification scenarios, which we call misclassification cost. This involves the use of specific values attached to each kind of misclassification, namely the false positives and false negatives. Beyond this, there can be other model-related heuristics that you can explore or even create to make your prediction models better. Finally, we looked at how you can leverage these heuristics and what you need to consider when using them.

In the chapter that follows, we'll look at some other heuristics to use in various aspects of the pipeline as well as beyond data science problems.

CHAPTER 8

Additional Heuristics

8.1 Overview of additional heuristics

In addition to the heuristics we discussed so far, there are other, more generic heuristics. After all, we do not always tie our work to a particular model or dataset. Sometimes, we just need to explore and analyze particular pieces of data before deciding what we could do with them. Heuristics can also add a lot of value since they are versatile enough to handle single variables or combinations of variables independent of each other. Such variables could be useful additions to a dataset, but we first need to understand them better and perform some data engineering tasks. That's what we will cover in this chapter.

We'll start by looking at entropy as well as ectropy (a lesser-known broad-scoped heuristic that is somewhat easier to work). Then we'll cover some distance-related heuristics (not to be confused with distance-based ones). We'll also examine how distance and similarity metrics are innately related and how to utilize them in transductive models and the confidence index heuristic. Next we'll talk about some important considerations we need to have regarding these heuristics to optimize their use in our work.

A codebook accompanies this chapter to allow you to reinforce your understanding of these concepts and make them your own. Maybe you can develop your own versions of them through this whole process. After all, these are just some but not all of the creativity tools for data work.

8.2 The Entropy and Ectropy heuristics

8.2.1 Entropy

Let's start our exploration of these heuristics with entropy, which is probably something you've heard of and even used somewhere. Entropy is a probabilistic heuristic and one of the most important metrics in information theory, with many applications in telecommunications. Also, it's been widely used in computer science and has brought about a series of useful tools, such as compression algorithms.

The objective of entropy is to figure out how much information there is in a piece of data by calculating how improbable its distribution. The idea is that the more predictable something is, the less (useful) information it conveys. For example, if you live in a northern city in the North hemisphere and someone tells you that it will be cloudy that winter day, that doesn't convey much information since most winter days in such a place are cloudy. If, however, that person tells you that it's going to be a completely sunny day, that statement is more information-rich. Entropy captures that sort of deviation from the expected through the use of probabilities using an elegant formula:

$$E = - \Sigma(p_i * \log(p_i))$$

where p_i is the probability of an event i happening, log() a logarithm operator (usually in base 2), and E the entropy of all that. Since entropy tends to be more holistic than that, we tend to sum up the various probability-based quantities on the right, hence the summation operator Σ. Note that since the logarithm of a probability will be either negative or zero, we use the minus sign (-) in the formula to ensure we end up with a positive result.

Entropy takes values between 0 and infinity, with higher values related to more disorder (unpredictability). That's why we view entropy as a measure of disorder.

Since we link entropy to information potential, it is a proxy for information in data-related fields. It's no coincidence that a heuristic called mutual information (I) is based on entropy and refers to the combination of two signals (variables).

8.2.2 Ectropy

Ectropy is a similar yet complementary heuristic to entropy. Some researchers have defined it as the reverse of entropy (hence the term *neg-entropy*), but if you are interested in more than a superficial approach to the concept, you may want to explore it more deeply. I've done this when delving into the concept of density, which we covered in the previous chapter. So, although ectropy captures the same signal as entropy, it uses densities rather than probabilities. Also, in its latest form, relative ectropy, this heuristic is bounded in the interval [0, 1], making it an easier metric to interpret. In specific, (absolute) ectropy is defined as follows, for any nominal variable x:

$$Ect = \frac{1}{k} \sum \left(\frac{k \cdot v}{n} - 1 \right)^2$$

where k is the number of unique values in x, v is the vector of frequencies for these unique values, and n is the total number of points in x.

For the relative version of ectropy, it's the same formula but divided by the following quantity, which is the highest possible ectropy of a categorical variable like that:

$$k \cdot (k-1) \cdot \left(1 - \frac{k}{n} \right)^2$$

This way, relative ectropy is always between 0 and 1, inclusive. What's more, just like entropy, ectropy has derivative metrics, such as one that handles a pair of variables and calculates the additional information the second one provides to the first. Note that for continuous variables, ectropy is still applicable. For this to work, however, the variable needs to be made discrete first. Fortunately, a few heuristics do just that, but they are quite complex and beyond the scope of this book. However, you can always use the binning method for making histograms the starting point.

8.2.3 Whether to use entropy or ectropy in a data-related problem

Both entropy and ectropy are useful and although highly correlated, they are somewhat complementary. So, the question naturally arises as to whether to use one or the other for a data-related problem. To answer this question, we need to consider scalability and the nature of the variables. If they are complex variables or they involve lots of data points, it would be better to use ectropy. On the other hand, if we plan to use heuristics from information theory in our work, entropy would be better.

In any case, it's good to keep in mind that they both have their limitations, so sometimes, there is no right answer to the question. After all, they are just heuristics, even if certain books like to idealize entropy, banking on its reputation as a powerful metric in physics, where it adds a lot of value to thermodynamics.

8.3 Distance-related heuristics

Let's now explore distance-related heuristics, namely distance and similarity metrics. This is a very important family of heuristics, yet complex because it's a relatively abstract topic. However, gaining a solid understanding of it can help you appreciate most transductive models and methods out there and discern when they are most applicable. For educational purposes, we'll split these heuristics into two broad categories: distance and similarity heuristics. However, keep in mind that they are part of the same family since the latter derives from the former in most cases.

8.3.1 Distance heuristics

Distance heuristics are very useful in analytics, particularly in geometry-based methods. As the computational power of computers these days is large enough, computing distances of millions of data points, even with the most sophisticated metrics, isn't a challenge nor a time-consuming task. Of course, we all have some penchant for the more-known distance metric taught in school, Euclidean distance, but there are so many other distance metrics that often put Euclidean distance to shame. After all, Euclid developed this metric for 2-D and 3-D geometry problems, not the often high-dimensional datasets we face!

Although I tried to keep the code as self-sufficient as possible without relying much on external libraries, it makes better sense to work with the Distances package in the case of distance heuristics. This library is both established and comprehensive, while it's fairly easy to use. If you wish to develop your own distance heuristic, you can always define it as a custom function and use it just like any other distance function in that library. For example, say that we want to use the inverse operators of the Euclidean distance in your metric, calculating distance using the formula:

$$d = \left(\sum \left(\sqrt{(|x - y|)} \right) \right)^2$$

you can define it using the following function (which is independent of the Distances package):

mydist(x::Vector{Real}, y::Vector{Real}) = (sum(sqrt.(abs.(x - y))))^2

Alternatively, you can view it as a special case of the Minkowski distance, with an m value of 0.5, using the corresponding function from the Distances package:

mydist(x::Vector{Real}, y::Vector{Real}) = minkowski(x, y, 0.5)

The key idea of distance heuristics is to help us handle peculiar scenarios for evaluating how different two points (or whole matrices) are. In the high-dimensional space, conventional metrics like the Euclidean distance or the Manhattan distance (also known as Cityblock distance) don't work so well, so we need to be creative. Fortunately, there are plenty of distance heuristics, most of which are supported by the Distances library. If you plan to use this library, it's best to check out its documentation for more information (https://github.com/JuliaStats/Distances.jl).

8.3.2 Similarity heuristics

Similarity heuristics are usually the inverse of a distance heuristic. Many people consider distances as similarities or a proxy for similarity. After all, if two data points are close to each other, they are similar for all practical purposes. This may not always be the case, though, since sometimes the distance metric is defined based on similarity. This proves that these two kinds of metrics are closely related.

A simple heuristic for transforming a distance metric into a similarity one is the following basic script:

$$\text{sim}(x, y) = 2 / (1 + \text{dist}(x, y) / d_{max}) - 1$$

where dist() is any distance heuristic metric and d_{max} is the maximum possible distance between any points in the space x and y dwell. This way, the distance between x and y is transformed into a similarity metric that is always between 0 and 1. Of course, figuring out the maximum distance d_{max} isn't always going to be easy, unless the data is normalized to begin with. If you can't bother with all the math involved, you can always find an approximation of d_{max} using a Monte Carlo simulation or something similar.

Similarity heuristics that don't depend on the distance between two points usually depend on some other quantity, such as the angle of the vectors corresponding to these points, as in the case of the cosine similarity heuristic. Since it would be largely redundant to have a whole new library just for the similarity heuristics, all of the most popular ones have been defined as distances. If you search in the metrics in the Distances library, you'll find the distance metric corresponding to the cosine similarity metric (i.e., the cosine distance).

Naturally, you can always develop your own similarity heuristics if the available ones don't help you enough for your data problem. For instance, say that the cosine similarity falls short because it only considers the angle between the vectors of the points at hand. What if it could factor in the difference in the length of these vectors too? That's something you may want to try out as an exercise and a way to hone your creativity!

8.3.3 Relationship to the confidence index

All this stuff about distances and similarities is great, but how does it apply to other areas of data science, such as data models? That's where the confidence index comes in handy, at least for the transductive models, which rely on distances/similarities for their predictions. Since the values of both of these heuristics work similarly, we'll refer to them as similarities. Specifically, we can use the distances to calculate the confidence index for a more accurate estimation of the validity of each prediction. In the case of a classification scenario using kNN, for example, we can calculate the confidence index as follows:

$$CI = s_{wc} / (s_{wc} + s_{oc})$$

where s_{wc} is the similarity of the winning class (i.e., the average similarity of all the neighbors of that class) and s_{oc} is the similarity of the other classes in the neighborhood examined. Clearly, we can also use this metric as the decision rule for the classification process itself. That's what one powerful version of kNN does, with generally better success than the original kNN classifier.

8.4 Important considerations

This chapter's alternative heuristics have their peculiarities, much like the other heuristics we explored in this book. For example, although there is a version of entropy that handles continuous variables, it's not as scalable as you would expect from such a simple heuristic. In any case, if you plan to work with continuous variables and need to evaluate their entropies, you can always apply a discretization method on them, just like you would do for the ectropy heuristic. However, certain such methods may not be good for this task. Binning, for example, manages to turn a variable into a categorical one. It does so in a way that diffuses its signal, so the corresponding entropy or ectropy evaluations are bound to be inaccurate. Generally, there is always information loss whenever you change a continuous variable to a discrete one since it is one-way (lossy) compression of sorts.

Distance heuristics are restricted by the dimensions of the data at hand. For example, as the number of dimensions increases, it negatively affects all of these metrics. This means that their value diminishes as the dimensionality increases, making many points seem very similar in terms of distance. Also, calculating these metrics may become problematic as many dimensions may cause an overflow issue in the memory registers that handle the variables at hand. So, it's often the case that we may need to perform dimensionality reduction first before leveraging these heuristics extensively. Nevertheless, there is also the possibility of an adaptive heuristic that can handle various dimensionalities, but that's a quite esoteric topic that's bound to not be of interest to most data science professionals.

Additionally, the similarity heuristics are bound by the same limitations of the distance heuristics. Still, they are also a bit off because they often fail to capture the full spectrum of the signal of the data at hand. The cosine similarity, for instance, although it's a brilliant heuristic, doesn't take into account the actual distance of the two points examined, merely the angle between them. So, even if it's useful in NLP problems for finding word or document similarity, it's not as broad in its scope as you would expect.

Finally, it's important to remember that you can always come up with newer and possibly better distance or similarity heuristics. Although many researchers in this area have expressed a great deal of creativity, it's doubtful that they have explored most of the possibilities out there. After all, most people who do research in this area aren't always looking for newer heuristics; the latter come about organically as they attempt to solve a complex problem in a novel way. Perhaps you too can follow in their footsteps.

8.5 Summary

We examined a few heuristics beyond the categories of the previous chapters, which are very useful in data-related work. Namely, we looked at entropy, ectropy, and distance-related heuristics, including the similarity heuristics that often stem from the latter. We saw that both entropy and ectropy can tell us a few things about the information content of a variable by analyzing how unlikely the various values of that variable are. Although they are primarily defined for categorical variables, they can also work on continuous ones, after these variables are turned into categorical ones in a proper fashion that maintains as much of their signal as possible. Additionally, we looked at the distance heuristics and their equivalent ones which are known as similarity metrics.

We examined how one can turn into another through an inversion process and how a similarity metric can even be bounded in the [0, 1] interval if we use the maximum possible distance, whenever this is feasible to calculate. Finally, we explored some useful considerations for all these heuristics, such as the fact that the scope of certain metrics, such as the cosine similarity, may be limited to NLP problems. Fortunately, the various limitations of these heuristics open the possibility of new ones, making the whole area of exploring this sort of heuristics a very creative process.

With these heuristics, we have completed the first part of our exploration in the world of heuristics. In the following chapters, we'll look into optimization-related heuristics and how they add value to our more specialized problem-solving endeavors.

PART III

Optimization-oriented Heuristics

By their very nature, heuristic shortcuts will produce biases, and that is true for both humans and artificial intelligence, but the heuristics of AI are not necessarily the human ones.

Daniel Kahneman

CHAPTER 9

Artificial Intelligence and Machine Learning Optimization

9.1 Optimization overview

The heuristics for AI are not necessarily like the heuristics we use in our human minds. After all, AI thinks differently, which is evident in how they tackle problems. If you've ever played against an AI in chess or some other strategy game, you're quite familiar with this point. Optimization is a methodology that helps us tackle many such scenarios, be it problems modeled mathematically or data-driven (machine learning). Even if you are not that fond of math or machine learning (ML), you can still learn and master this methodology and have a gentle entry into AI in the process. After all, there is an optimizer or two at the core of any AI system, while the more sophisticated optimizers are well within AI territory.

But what is optimization anyway, and why is it important? Most importantly, why would a data professional care about all this? For starters, optimization can help us solve many problems, including finding the best, or nearly the best, set of parameters for the data models we build. Also, optimization is our only choice to solve certain types of problems. Additionally, optimization can help us think differently in solving problems and creating new strategies for their solution. Furthermore, optimization is a powerful methodology whenever you need to find optimal values for something, be it a problem modeled mathematically, a data model, or anything else involving mathematical functions. Finally, it's also a popular approach to problem-solving in business since many problems involve minimizing cost, maximizing revenue, or minimizing attrition.

However, optimization doesn't just try to solve problems that mathematics professionals tackle with the various techniques calculus provides. These are all great, but they tend to be limited to certain kinds of functions:

- functions that are continuous (i.e., they don't have any gaps in their plots)
- functions that have a derivative, or two (i.e., you can find the rate of change of these functions in relation to the various variables they depend on)
- the number of variables involved is relatively small

The last point is very important since in the problems we encounter in our field, we often have to deal with many variables. Therefore, even if we can greatly reduce our datasets, the models may have many parameters that need to be optimized, since they often involve meta-features too, which they create. Also, most real-world problems tend to be quite complex, so conventional optimization methods just won't work! So learn and master these methods before the more sophisticated ones are covered in subsequent chapters.

This chapter will cover optimization in general, including use cases, the key components of an optimization algorithm (the optimizer), optimization's role in AI and ML, and important considerations. Unfortunately, no codebook accompanies this chapter, but feel free to play around with conventional optimizers if you feel like coding. Also, find some mathematical functions that you would like to experiment with using the optimization methods we'll cover. Don't worry if they are complicated—that's where modern optimizers excel!

9.2 Optimization use cases

Let's now take a look at a few of the most prominent use cases of optimization, focusing on the ones that are the biggest value-adds, such as logistics. Although most of the problems in this industry involve minimizing time or distance (or a combination of the two along with other factors, under the umbrella term "cost"), and are modeled with graphs, logistics problems often involve many variables and tackling them with conventional methods is practically unfeasible. Also, we save a lot of money and energy through optimization because the problems involved are recurrent ones, making the savings recurrent too. So, for example, optimization won't just get you that Amazon package faster, it will also mitigate the effect of delivery trucks on the environment (e.g. traffic, pollution, etc.).

Another use case where optimization adds value is data warehouse optimization. Even though fewer companies today have their own data centers compared to the previous decade, data warehouses can also live on a company's servers or even on the cloud. So, optimizing the various data flows and the overall architecture is no simple task. Although this kind of problem is something a data modeler would excel, it's good to know that we could at least help with its solution through the optimization methodology.

Finally, telecommunications is a frequent use case for optimization. This translates into Extract, Transform, and Load (ETL) practices in our field. However, it can involve all kinds of problems in the more general area, including satellite transmissions, cellular networks, and optic fiber infrastructure. In any case, it's a complex problem that often involves large investments and long-term projects, so optimization is not just useful but necessary. This is especially the case now when we have a great deal of satellite internet as potentially a viable alternative to conventional ISPs, at least for the more rural parts of the planet. Moreover, if we also consider the IoT infrastructure that seems to be growing steadily, it's clear that optimizing data logistics will be an increasingly important matter.

9.3 Key components of an optimization algorithm

Let's now explore the various components of an optimization algorithm to be on the same page. First of all, we have the objective function (the fitness function), which is the algorithm's objective. This is the mathematical function the optimizer attempts to maximize or minimize. Defining it properly is not the simplest task, though in some cases, when the business objective is clear, it's more straightforward.

The variables involved in the fitness variable are the independent variables the optimizer needs to work with to find the best (optimal) values so that the value of the objective function is maximum or minimum. These variables are independent, though the optimizer's function isn't influenced that much if they depend upon each other. If there are strong correlations among these variables, that's something you can harness to simplify the problem a bit, making things easier for the optimizers involved.

Beyond these components, which are essential for every optimization problem, there is an optional one too: the constraints (restrictions) set. These are many limitations for the variables of the problem that need to be taken into account by the optimizer. For example, we may want the variables to sum up to 1 in the case of weight coefficients. That can be formalized as a constraint: $w_1 + w_2 + \ldots w_n = 1$, where w_i is the i-th independent variable of the problem, and n is the total number of variables. Other constraints may have to do with the range of the variables. For instance, we may want the variables to have positive values, in which case we'd have a constraint like $w_i > 0$, for each i between 1 and n, inclusive. The constraints may complicate the optimization process, but they are often essential for properly modeling the problem and obtaining a useful solution.

Additional components of the optimization algorithm include the various parameters related to its function. These differ across optimizers but are also important since they impact the algorithm's performance. Usually, some default settings are available, which you can tweak if you aren't content with the performance or the optimizer results. We'll cover specific optimizers and their settings in the next few chapters.

9.4 Optimization's role in AI and ML

Let's now discuss optimization in artificial intelligence and machine learning. Although we won't detail these applications in this book, it's helpful to hone your perspective of optimization's value-add, especially its more evolving aspects.

Optimization is useful in large ANNs, also known as deep learning (DL) networks, where many parameters need to be optimized. Although conventional optimization algorithms work well, sometimes we need to train the DL network before the sun goes supernova—training a DL network can be quite time-consuming. Fortunately, that's something that the more advanced optimizers can provide. This is particularly the case for more sophisticated DL networks. Note that since these scenarios involve a lot of parameters, it's wise to use more advanced optimization algorithms. When using smaller ANNs, however, conventional optimizers will work fine.

Machine learning algorithms also use optimization to some extent, especially ensemble models. Even the humble decision tree model uses some optimization (some version of this popular model involves the entropy heuristic). As long as you can define the model's performance with a cost function or something equivalent, you can try to minimize that function using some optimization algorithm. A typical cost function in such a case could be the number of false positives and false negatives in a classification or the mean squared error in a regression problem. Usually, all this involves the training data, though sometimes a validation set is involved.

Optimizing parameters in a data model can be tricky since there is such a thing as optimizing too much. This can lead to the model overfitting, which is undesirable. However, if you pick the fitness function carefully, optimization can help significantly. It's best to understand existing optimizers in ML models before implementing your own. Understanding optimization's relationship to AI and ML is necessary if you decide to create your own models. The chances are that you'll need to include an optimization process somewhere in the fit() or train() function of that model. Although optimizers like Gradient Descent are quite decent and popular, they are just one of the many options for optimization algorithms, as we'll see in the next chapter.

9.5 Important considerations

Optimization is an NP-hard problem, particularly when dealing with constraints. For us non-computer scientists, finding the best solution is quite hard, and the complexity of the problem increases dramatically as the number of variables increases. Also, there are no shortcuts to finding the best solutions, at least not in terms of the algorithm involved. To get around that issue, we often rely on heuristics and compromise the quality of these solutions. We still don't solve the original NP-hard problem, but we find an approximation of its solution that's good enough for the end-user. So, we may not get the best possible solution for a given problem, but we'll get something close enough that works. We'll talk more about this kind of optimization in the next chapter.

Additionally, it's important to remember that sometimes the type of variables involved plays a crucial role in the optimization problem. For example, sometimes we are looking at integer variables, so a solution like $x^* = (2.4, 5.1, 9.9, 0.6)$ wouldn't be acceptable. Also, finding the optimal solution in such a scenario isn't as simple as rounding off since these rounding errors accumulate and greatly depend on the slopes in that region of the solution space. Therefore, it's best to opt for a particular optimizer geared towards integer inputs (discrete optimization) to tackle such scenarios.

Optimization requires a lot of computational resources, at least when the problem involves lots of variables and constraints. So, before executing the script that will give you a potential solution, make sure you are willing to allocate all these resources and wait for it to finish. Stopping it prematurely may be a waste of resources and time. Instead, perhaps you could simplify the problem a bit first or opt for a different optimization approach to better use your resources. Optimization may be a powerful methodology for problem-solving, but it's not a plug-and-play technique that you can assign to a beginner and then break for lunch!

Finally, some optimizers, especially the more advanced and modern ones, are stochastic, meaning that they involve some form of randomness. Because of this, the outputs they yield may be different from iteration to iteration, even if the inputs are the same. Therefore a good optimizer using a well-defined objective function may yield an inadequate solution. So try the optimization a few times and pick the solution that better minimizes or maximizes the objective function.

9.6 Summary

We started our optimization journey by looking at optimization as a methodology for finding the best solution to a problem defined mathematically and involves a set of variables and constraints. Then, we examined the value of optimization, particularly in industries like logistics, warehouse optimization, and telecommunications. There is a value-add in AI and ML, particularly in more complex models with lots of parameters that need to be managed for the training of these models. Next, we covered optimization considerations, including that optimization is an NP-hard problem, the importance of the variable type, the need for a lot of computational resources for large-scale optimization problems, and the fact that many optimizers are stochastic.

Next, we'll look at how heuristics can be a value-add in the optimization methodology. We'll also use a codebook to hopefully help make all the concepts we discussed already more concrete. Note that the focus on optimization will be on the more advanced optimizers, which are also the more interesting.

CHAPTER 10

Heuristics in Optimization

10.1 Heuristics in optimization in general

Just like any NP-hard problem, optimization is time-consuming, at least when the dimensionality of the problems increases. For example, it's fairly easy nowadays to find the absolute optimum solution for a problem having five or even ten variables. However, finding the absolute optimum solution isn't worth the computational resources when the dimensionality increases beyond that point. Also, the time required seems to increase exponentially with the number of variables and restraints often part of the optimization problem. So, what do we do?

We resort to heuristics once more, this time more complex ones involving whole algorithms, for tackling the optimization problem more creatively. Since we have solved these problems with this approach, a whole series of such heuristics can help us tackle all sorts of optimization problems, even highly complex ones.

This chapter will summarize some of these heuristics-based optimization algorithms. Then we'll focus on Particle Swarm Optimization (PSO) and explore how it employs heuristics and how the whole algorithm is like a heuristic itself. We'll also look at some important considerations regarding optimization heuristics, including the PSO algorithm. Accompanying this chapter is a Neptune notebook that has an implementation of PSO and a few examples of how it is applied. After going through the notebook, try out some new things, such as using alternative fitness functions and parameter values.

10.2 Specific optimization algorithms using heuristics

There are four categories of optimization algorithms based on heuristics:

- Swarm-based algorithms (such as PSO)
- Genetic algorithms
- Simulated annealing and similar algorithms
- Other heuristics-based optimizers

Let's look at each one of these groups. Most of these optimization algorithms are often referred to as nature-inspired algorithms since they borrow ideas found in nature, mimicking some of the processes observed in the wild. The most apparent such group is the swarm-based ones, which imitate the movement of swarms of various insects.

10.2.1 Swarm-based algorithms

You may be looking at this subsection title and wonder what do swarms have to do with optimization? After all, optimization is all about mathematical functions, right? Well, it is, but each potential solution to these problems is essentially a point in the n-dimensional space that represents all possible solutions (from now on, we'll refer to this as the solutions space of the problem). So if we were to track down one of these solutions as it changes (evolves), we'd observe a movement resembling an insect. And if we were to track down multiple such solutions moving simultaneously, all while influencing each other's movements, we'd be looking at a swarm.

Using a swarm instead of a single solution is probably the most innovative one in optimization history. Swarm represents a leap in our thinking, since we don't put all our eggs in one basket and instead count on a collection of possibilities. The financial equivalent is having a portfolio of investments instead of putting all your money into a single investment. For the long term, such a strategy should perform well, with sufficient confidence, unless the whole market crashes. The same goes for the swarm-based optimization algorithms, which rely on various potential solutions working together or in a complementary fashion, to obtain an overall good result. That is, the optimum value of the fitness function. We'll look into one such algorithm in the next section of this chapter and the codebook that accompanies this chapter.

10.2.2 Genetic algorithms

Genetics has been an up-and-coming field over the past decades, one that put biology on the map. However, the genetics these algorithms employ do not involve DNA per se, but rather strings of characters or numbers, representing potential solutions to an optimization problem (a kind of informational DNA). Since there are a bunch of such algorithms based on the same concept, we often refer to this approach as genetic algorithms (GAs). This is also probably one of the most developed families of optimization algorithms and one that's bound to evolve further.

Originally, GAs were poised to solve discrete optimization problems, and at one point, they became famous for tackling the Traveling Salesman Problem (TSP) better than any other optimizer out there. TSP is an NP-hard problem involving the typical logistics scenario of a single salesperson who needs to travel around a certain area, going through each one of the main cities once and returning to the starting point where he presumably lives. Since time is money, he doesn't want to spend more time on the road than necessary. He could plot his course optimally for a few cities, but when the number of cities increases, the only way to solve this problem efficiently is through a heuristics-based optimizer.

GAs can also tackle problems involving continuous variables, though the precision of the solution may make the parameters of the algorithm more demanding when it comes to computational resources. Speaking of parameters, that's a different ball game for newcomers to this optimization approach. There are many of them, and it's not easy to pick the best values since they are often problem-dependent. GAs also deal with a collection of potential solutions that evolve together, though quite different from the swarm-based optimizers. In the next chapter, we'll talk more about GAs, covering complex optimization scenarios that lend themselves to this approach.

10.2.3 Simulated annealing and variants

This optimizer has been around for over 70 years, though it was recognized as an independent optimizer in the 1980s. Inspired by the natural phenomenon of physical annealing, a thermodynamics term referring to the cooling of liquids to form crystals, Simulated Annealing (SA) takes this concept and applies it to mathematical functions to find their optima. Also, unlike the previous two categories of optimizers, this one uses a single solution that evolves over time.

In the book "AI for Data Science" (Technics Publications) we describe this optimization algorithm as follows: "At the core of the annealing process emulated by SA is temperature: a control parameter for the whole process. Temperature starts with a fairly high value (such as 10,000 degrees), and then it gradually falls, usually at a geometric rate. Through all this, the energy level of the liquid also falls as it gradually takes a solid form. This represents the value of the fitness function, which is generally minimized (although maximization is also possible). As the temperature is relatively high, larger changes in the search space are possible; this makes exploring more potential solutions feasible, at least at the beginning of the process. Once the temperature gets lower, exploration is diminished, as the method favors exploitation of the search space; later, the algorithm prefers to refine the solutions discovered."

Without being too complicated and with very few parameters, you may think this optimization method is fairly trivial and not worth mentioning alongside the previous ones. However, it does one thing very well: *it avoids local optima*, which can be a real issue in complex solution spaces. However, it's not without its problems since fine-tuning the parameters involved isn't easy. Although most optimization algorithms, like those mentioned previously, have a set of default values for their operational parameters, SA doesn't. This makes it more difficult to use for someone new to this optimization approach.

Since we won't be covering SA in this book, it seems a good compromise to at least include its pseudo-code in case you wish to implement it or merely study it. This excerpt from the "AI for Data Science" book covers it adequately:

1. *Define the optimization mode (minimization or maximization), initial temperature, temperature decrease rate, radius of neighborhood for each variable, and initial solution vector.*
2. *Propose an updated solution in the same neighborhood and evaluate it using the fitness function.*
3. *Accept updates that improve this solution.*
4. *Accept some updates that don't improve this solution. This "acceptance probability" depends on the temperature parameter.*
5. *Drop the temperature.*
6. *Repeat steps 2-5 until the temperature has reached zero, or a predefined minimum temperature.*
7. *Output the best solution found.*

10.2.4 Other

Beyond the aforementioned heuristics-based optimization methods, there are several others that you can explore on your own. If you are creative enough, you may even create your own optimizers. However, it's not as easy as coming up with a basic or even an advanced EDA heuristic. Developing a whole new metaheuristic is much more challenging, especially if it's something that solves a certain category of problems better than the existing optimizers. In fact, such a venture might be a solid PhD topic that would require a lot of math and a lot of programming. As a result, covering this sort of topic is way beyond the scope of this book. Still, it's good to mention that since the domain of optimization isn't limited to these or any other categories of algorithms and it's an active field of research.

10.3 Particle swarm optimization and heuristics

10.3.1 Overview

Let's now zero in on particle swarm optimization, which is probably one of the most interesting and most researched swarm-based optimizers. The original swarm-like optimizer inspired other, newer optimizers, such as Firefly, which we cover in "AI for Data Science".

PSO is a simple swarm-based algorithm, where the swarm members are called *particles*. There are N particles in the swarm, and that's one of the main parameters of the method. Although some users of PSO would set a constant value for N for all sorts of problems (e.g., 50), I've discovered that by making N depend on the number of variables in the problem (e.g., N = 10nv, where *nv* is the number of variables), the method yields somewhat better results. After all, more complex problems require more particles to cover the larger solutions space. You can call that a heuristic, though it's not part of the original algorithm. The algorithm takes these N particles and places them at random positions (part of the stochastic nature of the optimizer), then moves them around for *ni* iterations, and then spits out the result. The latter is the position of the best-performing particle and the value it corresponds to when it's inserted into the objective function.

Note that *ni* is best when large, even if this makes for slower performance. To balance that, we can include another parameter called *iwp*, which stands for iterations without progress. So, if the algorithm's best solution does not improve noticeably over iwp iterations, the algorithm stops even if it hasn't reached the ni-th iteration. Note that iwp is not in the original algorithm, but worth adding since it doesn't affect negatively the performance of the algorithm.

10.3.2 Pseudocode of PSO algorithm

If you prefer a more programmatic view of PSO, here is the pseudocode for it, as described by Dr. Eberhart and Dr. Kennedy in their paper from 1995[1] where they first introduced it:

For each particle in the swarm
    Initialize particle by setting random values to its initial state
End
Do
    For each particle in the swarm
        Calculate fitness value
        If the fitness value is better than the best fitness value in its history (pBest):
         pBest ← fitness value of particle
    End
    gBest ← particle with the best fitness value of all the particles in the swarm
    For each particle
        Calculate particle velocity according to equation A
        Update particle position according to equation B
    End
Repeat Until maximum iterations are reached OR minimum error criteria is attained

---

[1]   Kennedy, J. and Eberhart, R. (1995) Particle Swarm Optimization. Proceedings of IEEE International Conference on Neural Networks, Vol. 4, 1942-1948. http://dx.doi.org/10.1109/icnn.1995.488968.

10.3.3 Heuristics used

PSO uses two clever heuristics to adapt the swarm of solutions to the new information acquired through its wandering in the solution space. These correspond to the c parameter, a vector in our optimizer implementation (see codebook). In the original algorithm, it's two values, $c1$ and $c2$, which correspond to how much each particle is influenced by:

1. its own best position, and
2. the best-performing particle in the swarm.

We use these two parameters and some random numbers generated on the fly to calculate each particle's velocity in the solution space. We also use another parameter, *maxv*, to cap these velocities, so they don't get too high (resulting in erratic behavior of the swarm). The velocity of each particle helps us calculate its new position. We are working with discrete time here, with each time unit being an iteration of the algorithm.

Now, you may think that all this randomness in the algorithm might make it unstable and result in chaotic behavior. Counter-intuitively, it makes it more robust and able to handle local optima. That is, solutions that appear good in relation to their neighborhood in the solution space but aren't very good overall. Of course, the randomness causes the algorithm to output different results every time it's run, but these results tend to be very close to each other If they aren't, there is something wrong with the parameters used, so it's not PSO's fault. You can find an interesting visualization of the algorithm on TowardsDataScience: https://towardsdatascience.com/particle-swarm-optimization-visually-explained-46289eeb2e14.

To say that PSO is brilliant is an understatement since its elegance can be surpassed only by its efficiency in tackling many optimization problems. There is even an application of it in optimizing the weights of an ANN, from back when I was doing my PhD. So, if I don't stop myself now, I may fill up the rest of the book with PSO-related facts and anecdotes. Suffice to say that even if you end up writing a paper about PSO variants, like I did back in early 2010s, you are still scratching the surface of what this optimizer has in store. So, if you are interested in exploring it further, the best way to do so would be to study its implementation in the codebook and explore how you can potentially improve it or play around with it on various optimization scenarios.

10.4 Important considerations

Although the topic of heuristics in optimization seems straightforward from the birds-eye view we have had in this chapter, it's good to have certain things in mind. This is particularly useful if you decide to delve into this topic further, perhaps through some programming explorations in the sandbox of the codebook accompanying this chapter.

First of all, although some heuristics we covered may seem relevant to optimization, the chances are that they don't apply so well since they were designed for different problems. It's generally better to use heuristics designed for optimization if you want them to perform well and add value to your problem-solving efforts of this type. Of course, if you come up with a lightweight heuristic applicable everywhere (the Holy Grail of heuristics), you may want to give it a shot in this kind of problem-solving. Just manage your expectations before you set off to such an endeavor, though, since heuristics like the *diversity* one come once in a blue moon (we'll talk more about that heuristic in the next part of this book).

What's more, if you are unsure which heuristics-based optimization algorithm to use for a (complex) problem, you may want to try out different ones. If none of them work well enough, you may want to tinker with their parameters a bit. Every optimization problem is relatively unique, just like the data analytics problems, so it's good to remember that when you try to solve them. The one-size-fits-all approach may not work that well or save you time.

Additionally, PSO is sensitive to the parameters involved like other heuristics-based optimizers. The default values of $c1 = c2 = 2.0$ and $maxv = 2.0$ are fine as a starting point and yield decent results for most problems. However, if the convergence is quite long (the algorithm runs slowly), you may want to change them. Note, however, that high parameters values may make the algorithm erratic and unable to converge or come up with a good solution. This is a characteristic of the trade-off between speed and accuracy in most modern optimization algorithms.

Moreover, although PSO is quite mature and well-established, it's not without its limitations. Without being an optimization expert, one can develop variants where one or more heuristics are added to the core algorithm, making it more accurate or robust against complex solution spaces. The speed may suffer a bit as a result, but often this is a worthy compromise, at least for the more challenging optimization problems. After all, a compromise like this isn't too expensive, computationally speaking, and is worth it in the long term.

Furthermore, although PSO and other heuristics-based optimizers found in the scientific literature are quite mature and are treated with reverence by all those who understand them, it's good to remember that they started as creative projects. Their creators had no idea how successful these algorithms would be as optimizers, though they might have had aspirations tied to the success of these algorithms. So, if you have a good idea for a heuristic in the optimization arena, you may want to give it a shot. At the very least, you'll learn something and better understand the field overall.

Finally, just like every heuristic out there, PSO has its scope, even if various variants enable it to tackle many problems. Usually, each variant would tackle a specific shortcoming of the original PSO algorithm, extending its applicability to relevant problems. Still, it's better to opt for an alternative optimizer for discrete optimization problems. Genetic algorithms can be one such alternative, as we'll explore in the next chapter. So, if you like PSO, you'll probably like GAs too, perhaps even more than PSO.

10.5 Summary

We looked at heuristics in optimization from a holistic perspective. For starters, we looked at heuristics in optimization in general and how they have brought about a series of optimizers, particularly equipped for complex optimization problems. We also saw the main families of heuristics-based optimizers and how each is somewhat different in its approach to modeling and tackling a problem. Some of them are more specialized for specific problems (e.g., discrete variables), even if they can handle scenarios beyond their specializations. Additionally, we examined the overall pseudo-code of simulated annealing. We also looked at the particle swarm optimization algorithm and how it depends on heuristics for its brilliant and efficient functionality. Finally, we explored some important considerations, including that all these optimizers have their own scope, PSO has lots of interesting variants that extend its functionality, and that for more specialized problems involving discrete variables, it's sometimes better to resort to a different optimizer altogether.

Next, we'll discuss a family of such optimizers that are ideal for discrete optimization problems and other highly complex scenarios, namely genetic algorithms.

CHAPTER 11

Complex Optimization Systems

11.1 Complex optimizers overview

Recall the pop culture adage "modern problems require modern solutions." We cannot use conventional optimization tools to solve today's optimization problems. We need complex optimizers, especially for AI-related work. Complex optimizers involve a more sophisticated approach to finding the optima hidden in the solutions space. They may employ more than one strategy and several heuristics, like the PSO method we examined previously. It's not uncommon for someone to spend a whole PhD researching one such optimization method just so that he can make an improvement. Fortunately, you don't need to have a PhD in optimization or be a math expert to understand and implement such an algorithm.

This chapter will look at one such complex optimization method, namely the genetic algorithms (GAs) family of optimizers. We'll examine the heuristics involved in GAs and how they make a simple idea like the one GAs are based on into something sophisticated and intelligent enough to tackle complex problems. We'll examine in practice how they tackle one such problem in the codebook that accompanies this chapter. Moreover, we'll look at some important considerations when using GAs.

To get an idea of what kind of problems are suitable for the GAs approach, let's consider the case of a grid of cities that need to be connected by a network of highways (see Fig. 11.1).

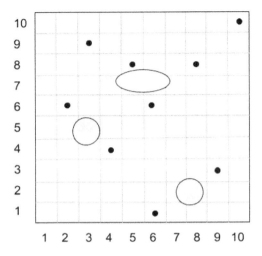

Fig. 11.1 A sample problem that lends itself to advanced optimizers, especially when the scale increases. This problem is solved using GAs in the codebook related to this chapter.

Natural obstacles (constraints) often need to be taken into account, since it's not a good idea to violate a natural park or a lake if there are other alternatives. After all, we just need to connect all the cities with as few highway miles as possible (so, most cities will not be directly connected to each other). The solution to this problem may be something you can work out on your own, but imagine if instead of nine cities, we have 90 or 900. That's when optimization methods like GAs would come in handy!

11.2 The genetic algorithms family of optimizers

Let's start our exploration of this category of optimization methods through the GAs family of optimizers. We'll begin with some key concepts throughout the GAs realm, discuss the vanilla flavor genetic algorithm (the standard genetic algorithm), and cover its limitations and variations. There are plenty more members of this family of algorithms, but most of them are of research interest primarily and generally not all that interesting for real-world applications. Still, we'll mention a couple of them, just in case someone is interested in researching this topic further.

11.2.1 Key concepts of GAs

Let's begin our exploration of GAs by examining the key concepts of this optimization approach. First of all, the whole GAs ecosystem follows these five tenets:

1. Each individual (potential solution) is in continuous competition with other solutions, with which it sometimes mates to create new solutions.
2. Each individual's fitness is evaluated based on the fitness function of the problem at hand.
3. The most successful individuals (based on their fitnesses) are selected and merged to create offspring—new individuals that inhabit the population from that generation.
4. The components (genes) of the fittest individuals propagate throughout the generation, gradually improving the "genetic pool" of the population, leading to better solutions over time.
5. Generally, each successive generation is more suitable for the environment and therefore yields a better solution.

Note that "generation" is the same as "iteration" in the PSO sense of the word. Also, there is a direct correspondence between "individual" and "particle". At the same time, the fitness function in both cases plays the same role, even if it takes different inputs because of the particular coding schema used in each method. Each individual is often referred to as a *chromosome* and corresponds to a particular solution to the problem. Each chromosome contains several *genes*, which are the variables (often binary) that make up the potential solution. The *population* is the collection of all the individuals/chromosomes and tends to remain the same size throughout the optimization process.

There are three main operators involved in GAs that help select and change solutions over time, from one generation to the next:

1. <u>Selection</u>. This means that the individuals with higher fitness scores are more likely to make it to the next generation (in part) by being selected as mating partners. There are various strategies for selection, with the simplest one being a roulette wheel based on the fitness scores of the various individuals as potential places for the ball to land. This is one area where the algorithm uses randomness.

2. <u>Crossover</u>. This involves the mating between two individuals. Once the algorithm selects a couple of chromosomes through the previous process, a subset of their genes is selected randomly and placed into a new chromosome, namely the offspring. The size of that chromosome is the same as that of each parent. There are various strategies for this to happen, with the simplest being to divide the chromosome of parent A in two and take a random half to combine with the complementary part from parent B. This whole process is also highly random.

3. <u>Mutation</u>. This involves the change of a random gene (or genes) to add more variety to the population's genome. In practice, this enables the population to diversify enough to avoid premature convergence, leading to sub-optimal results (i.e., a local optimum). Although the previous two operators always take place at the end of a generation, the mutation may not occur at all or only in certain generations. Just like the other operators, this one is highly random too.

11.2.2 The vanilla flavor GA and its limitations

Let's start putting all this together with the vanilla flavor GA, where it all started for the GAs realm. In a nutshell, the algorithm follows this logic:

1. Initialization. Create a population p with a random set of chromosomes
2. For each individual in population, calculate its fitness, using the fitness function
3. Repeat until convergence happens:

    a. Select parents from population, based on fitness values calculated previously

    b. Crossover and generate new individuals to constitute the population of the next generation

    c. Perform mutation to one or more individuals (with a given probability)

    d. Calculate fitness for each individual of the new population

We can find the best-performing individual for each generation and store that information (the individual with the best fitness score). We observe convergence when the new population best doesn't improve more than a given threshold (defined beforehand) over a number of consecutive generations. Otherwise, the algorithm runs until we reach the predefined number of generations, in which case it yields the best-performing chromosome and its corresponding fitness score.

We can code each chromosome in whatever way makes sense for the problem. In the simplest scenarios, it can be a series of binary values—in essence, the chromosome is a binary variable. In other cases, it can be a series of characters or strings. The chromosome can even comprise digits (in the case of a continuous function that needs to be optimized). Although in some cases it's a simple task, in more complex problems, the coding of the solution into a chromosome is a challenging task that takes planning to do properly.

11.2.3 Elitism variant

This simple variant is so fundamental that it makes one wonder why it wasn't included in the original GA. It states that we always keep the n best-performing (fittest) individuals in every generation, no matter what. Sometimes instead of an absolute number, we use a proportion of the population size. So, even if a parent individual performs better than an offspring, that chromosome remains in the population even if it's an old-timer compared to the newer individuals. Of course, the analogy with the original idea of a single species living in an ecosystem in an evolutionary manner starts to break down if we consider the consequences of this variant. In essence, it's possible (though not very likely) for an individual to be immortal, living through multiple generations. But if that's what it takes for the algorithm to work better and yield a good solution, why not? We'll cover elitism in the GA implemented in the codebook of this chapter.

11.2.4 Scaling hack

Since elitism is not part of the original GA, it is a variant. You can even call it a heuristic. Scaling has to do with the values of the fitness function for the various individuals of the population so that they are more spread out or closer together. Depending on the mathematical function you use for scaling, you can end up with fitness values that make more sense for the selection process. In any case, we normalize the various fitness values after they are scaled to add up to 1. This has to do with the roulette-like selection process, so having all the fitness values add up to 1 is necessary. After all, the random numbers involved tend to follow the uniform distribution, taking values between 0 and 1.

11.2.5 Constraints tweak

It's quite interesting that the original GA doesn't even have a constraints option. Fortunately, that's something you can easily add through this tweak of the fitness function. Say, for example, that you have a problem that involves figuring out the optimal connectivity among various cities. You are building a network of highways and you want to use as little concrete as possible. This lends itself as an optimization problem to be tackled through GAs, by depicting the cost as a function of the distance between each pair of cities. However, in some cases, having a highway between two cities isn't feasible, either because of physical obstacles between them or because the area in-between is occupied by a protected area such as a national park. Recall Fig. 11.1. This constitutes a constraint for the problem since any solution that involves a connection between such a pair of cities wouldn't be possible. So, you can tweak the fitness function to have a very high cost for that connection. Note that "very high" involves a finite number. Otherwise, this may cause the algorithm to fail to converge since a few chromosomes will have a fitness function of 0. We'll look into such a scenario in the codebook of this chapter.

11.2.6 Other variants

These hacks and tweaks are great for making the original GA better, but what about more sophisticated variants? There are a few of those too, which we'll briefly mention.

The Hybrid Genetic Algorithms (HGAs) are an ensemble comprising a GA for the global search and another optimizer (usually one involving derivatives) for a more local search. Once the GA starts to converge and no longer improves its solutions much. This hybrid approach enables us to find a good solution and do so faster and more accurately. HGAs are a great option if we can differentiate the fitness function or if an accurate solution is required.

The Self-Organizing Genetic Algorithm (SOGA) is another variant whereby the GA works not just on the problem at hand but on itself too. In particular, it optimizes its own parameters and the variables of the problem, saving you the trouble of fine-tuning the algorithm yourself. So, in a sense, SOGA qualifies as an AI system, though it's more likely to be a component of an AI system also.

Another variant worth considering is the Variable Selective Pressure Model (VSPM). This involves a more sophisticated selection strategy to guarantee a certain level of diversity in the population by using the concept of an "infant mortality rate." This concept involves an interesting tactic whereby the weaker chromosomes in the population don't make it to the next generation (like infants born with some mortal defect in a pre-industrial culture), leaving room for more robust chromosomes.

Genetic Programming (GP), although more like a methodology than a simple GA, can be viewed as a variant of sorts, though a quite specialized one. GP involves building a synthetic function off other simpler functions modeled as genes. The data involved for the optimization isn't a fitness function but more like a pair of data streams, one for the inputs and one for the desired outputs of the synthetic function. This is like a combination of a regression algorithm and an ANN. However, it manages to have more complexity than regressors and more transparency than any conventional ANN. However, GP isn't that easy to use, and if you don't know what you are doing, you can easily create a function that's an overfit solution.

11.3 Heuristics involved in genetic algorithms

If heuristics are like wild salmon, genetic algorithms are like a river network. Even if PSO lends itself to all sorts of tweaks using heuristics, often leading to new optimization algorithms altogether, GAs do that but on a whole new level. Someone could argue that GAs are where heuristics thrive the most, at least in the field of optimization.

Specifically, we have the heuristic used for the selection operator, involving the fitness scores. This creates a fair system for picking a good individual for the mating process. Obviously, we could rank all the individuals and pick the top ones, but this would make the algorithm biased towards those high-performing ones, gradually eliminating all the other ones. This may be good at first but it's quite likely that it would make the optimizer converge to a local optimum. So instead, the selection heuristic ensures some diversity, and every individual has a chance of getting its genes to the next generation.

Another heuristic we encounter in GAs is of merging two different potential solutions (crossover). This ensures some diversity in the possibilities that come about since there is a lot of randomness. Moreover, this simple rule enables the optimizer to explore regions of the solutions space that would otherwise be inaccessible. Also, the new solutions are likely to be different enough to be useful, without being too similar to the previous solutions or too "out there" in relation to those same solutions.

What's more, the mutation heuristic is also employed, enabling the solutions to avoid getting stagnant. Even if we find a good solution, it may remain the same without the occasional (random) mutation since there may not be other solutions to lend it their genes. So, just like in the real world, various organisms mutate over time. The solutions in the GAs world follow the same pattern and enable the optimizer to explore those minor variations.

Naturally, we can consider the elitism variant a heuristic, perhaps even an essential one. Without adding too much computational burden to the algorithm, it ensures that at least some of the great solutions the optimizer has found can make it to the next generation. Of course, at least some of them will mate and make their genes linger in the population's gene pool, but what if their offspring isn't all that great? So, preserving a small number of individuals intact in the next generation, for every generation, is a wise move. The elitism heuristic enables that, even if it may slightly slow down the evolutionary process. However, if you overdo it with elitism, the optimizer will get trapped in the local optima those elite individuals represent, making convergence difficult, if not entirely unfeasible.

Finally, the scaling hack is a heuristic that makes selection fairer. This simple mathematical operator enables some justice among the various individuals when mating season comes. For example, it may be the case that some individuals' fitness scores are orders of magnitude higher than the rest, making them the only mating candidates that stand a chance. Clearly, this would break the selection process since they would be picked all the time. The scaling hack remedies that by balancing out the various fitness scores, still preserving their ranking, using a function like sqrt() or log(). In the reverse scenario, when the differences among the fitness scores are very small (almost negligible), you can use scaling with a different function, such as exp(), enabling those scores to diversify quite a bit.

This can make selection more meaningful since the various individuals won't be all the same, like the Smurfs.

11.4 Important considerations

Hopefully, you didn't get too excited about GAs so far because they can also be tricky, if not frustrating, initially. The many options they offer can make settling for a specific variation and a particular set of parameter values challenging. So, if you are looking for something simple, this is not where you'll find it—you might want to go back to PSO or even simulated annealing and make sure you master them first. If you are serious about GAs, it's best to start with ready-made code for specific examples that you understand and then work toward more challenging variations and problems.

Additionally, even though the standard genetic algorithm (what we refer to as vanilla flavor GA due to its conventional taste) may seem simple and easy to use, it's probably one of the worst GAs in existence. It's truly remarkable how something so limited and problematic gave rise to the splendor of the GAs family. So, if you plan to use that original GA, don't (unless it's just for getting a grasp of the main concepts involved in this family of optimizers).

What's more, just because GAs are powerful doesn't mean that they always work well. They are very fragile since their dependence on the initial conditions (parameters) is high, so if they don't yield a good enough result, don't blame them or your computer. It could be that they need some tweaking, perhaps one of the hacks we discussed previously. You can get them to work, though it's good to start with the default parameters and work around them initially.

Furthermore, just like PSO, GAs are ideal in scenarios where we cannot differentiate the fitness function, or the process of differentiating is very expensive computationally. Nevertheless, if you have easy access to the derivatives of the fitness function, other, more conventional optimization methods may be more effective for finding an accurate solution. Also, as we saw briefly in the variants section, you can always combine both the GAs and that derivatives-based optimizer in a hybrid setting for even better results.

Finally, how you encode a problem is paramount if you tackle it with GAs (the same goes for other advanced optimization methods, to some extent). Sometimes, a quick-and-dirty encoding schema may save you time at first but may lead to a more challenging problem for the GAs to solve. This is bound to result in an inaccurate solution. Think about how to best encode the problem, perhaps using some creativity, before handing it off to the GAs to tackle.

11.5 Summary

We explored the main aspects of the genetic algorithms family of optimizers as an example of a complex optimization system. Specifically, we looked at how complex optimization systems have to do with a sophisticated approach to finding the optima in the solutions space, often dealing with constraints and other limitations. Additionally, we looked at the GAs family of optimizers as an example of complex optimizers. The original (vanilla flavored) GA is fairly simple and may not yield amazing results, but through a series of tweaks and add-ons, it gives rise to a whole set of similar algorithms that have a more robust performance and yield more accurate results. All GAs involve some key operators such as selection, crossover, and mutation. Moreover, we examined how GAs use heuristics to find the sought-after optima in problems. The aforementioned operators are some such heuristics, as well as the elitism and scaling one. Finally, we looked at a few important considerations about GAs.

In the following chapter, we'll examine optimization ensembles and how different optimizers can tackle a problem in tandem. Then, without getting too technical, we'll see how heuristics can add value to optimization tasks and better understand what intelligence is all about, at least in the problem-solving arena.

CHAPTER 12

Optimization Ensembles

12.1 Optimization ensembles overview

We can combine optimizers in an ensemble setting like predictive data models. By working together, they can yield a better (more accurate) solution or, perhaps, come up with an adequate solution faster. Nevertheless, this isn't an easy task, so few people in this field talk about this optimization system. After all, optimization heuristics are complex enough by themselves, so coming up with more complex heuristics that have other groups of heuristics as their components isn't something most optimization professionals are able or willing to do.

Optimization ensembles are often referred to as *hybrid systems* in the scientific literature. However, we prefer to avoid adding another term to AI-related optimization's vast lexicon when *ensemble* works well as a general descriptor. Besides, this is the term most commonly used in the industry since it's the same term used to describe a functional combination of data models.

In this chapter, we'll explore the topic of optimization ensembles in some depth, starting with the structure of an optimization ensemble. Then, we'll proceed to examine the role of heuristics in optimization ensembles before we look at some important considerations about these optimization systems. This chapter doesn't have a codebook accompanying it, but you are welcome to create your own or supplement the previous one to explore further the ideas presented in this chapter.

12.2 Structure of an optimization ensemble

An optimization ensemble is like a meta-optimizer of sorts. In other words, it's a more complex optimization algorithm that has other optimizers as its components. This excerpt from the book "AI for Data Science" (Technics Publications) describes it quite well:

Optimization ensembles combine the performances of various optimization systems that tackle the same problem. These systems may be iterations of the same method, with different parameters and/or starting values, or they can comprise different methods altogether. Alternatively, optimization ensembles can exchange data from one optimizer to another, in an attempt to further improve accuracy of the results. Naturally, this approach requires a more in-depth understanding of the methods involved, as well as more fine-tuning each solution to the problem at hand.

Normally, the optimization ensemble would deploy all these optimizers to dedicated workers on the computer or network the ensemble would run on. This framework is referred to as parallelism (with cluster computing being a popular form) and is used across various data science applications. In any case, we would structure the optimization ensemble as shown in Figure 12.1.

Fig. 12.1 A diagram of a basic optimization ensemble. Note that the fitness function is the same in both, and that we compare the optimizers' outputs before the ensemble yields a single output. In this diagram, the circle node signifies merging the two signals yielded by the two optimizers. This merging takes place using a basic operator like min() or max(), depending on the optimization mode. Naturally, there can be any number of optimizers involved in this setup.

In general, there would be a main method that would be the master worker of the group, akin to the reduce node of a map-reduce setup. This method would be responsible for coordinating the various optimizers and combining their outputs. Each of these optimizers could work either independently or using the outputs of another optimizer, like nodes of an ANN across various layers. How exactly it would function would depend on the architecture and its master algorithm. The various optimizers can be of the same algorithm (e.g., various instances of PSO), or different ones (e.g., a PSO, a Firefly, an Ant Colony Optimizer, etc.).

It's important to note that the ensemble would run as long as at least one optimizer/worker node is active. For this purpose, it would make sense to fine-tune the various optimizers to complete their task at comparable times so that no one, especially the master worker, would have to wait too long to do its task. That's why sometimes it's better to use instances of the same optimization algorithms across the various worker nodes of the optimization network.

12.3 Role of heuristics in optimization ensembles

Optimization ensembles are often heavily dependent on heuristics, though this doesn't mean the former have to comprise heuristics-based optimizers. You can have an optimization ensemble with all sorts of optimizers as its components, though the chances are that it would be better if there were at least one heuristics-based optimizer. Combining these optimizers depend on the problem complexity, including the number of variables involved and the landscape of the solutions space.

In optimization ensembles, simpler heuristics are often good enough. For example, you can have one to use as a termination condition for any optimizers involved. If, for instance, an optimizer doesn't make progress over a certain predefined threshold (often depicted as the *tolerance* constant), that optimizer may be forced to stop. Note that this heuristic can be used in any optimizer and doesn't require the optimizer to be part of an ensemble. However, suppose the optimizer is used in an ensemble. In that case, this heuristic is necessary since you wouldn't want to have that optimizer running needlessly while the rest of the network waits for it to finish. This is particularly the case when using parallelism.

We can use different heuristics to combine the results of the various optimizers. The simplest one would be to get the highest or lowest value and the corresponding solution. That is, the best-performing optimizer's outputs. For different optimizers which yield very similar but not identical solutions, you can also take the average of these solutions (e.g., using the median metric) and then calculate the corresponding fitness score of that average. The final result may be even better than any of the outputs of the individual optimizers.

Beyond these simple heuristics, you can use more sophisticated ones, such as an optimizer to figure out the best parameter values of the individual optimizers, much like someone would do in a data model hyper-parameter optimization scenario. This may be more time-consuming and resource-heavy, but in some cases, it may be worth it as a strategy. Also, you can have another heuristic for figuring out how to partition the search space to optimize the parallel search of the various optimizers of the ensemble.

Have a good set of multi-dimensional random numbers as your initial solution regardless of your strategy. This is particularly useful in cases involving continuous variables. Coming up with such a set of random solutions that are organically diverse is not easy, as the conventional randomness-related functions in some off-the-shelf library may not be good enough. However, they may be sufficient for other applications.

12.4 Important considerations

There is a reason why optimization ensembles are not currently mainstream, and that has to do with various issues with using them. For starters, just like in data model ensembles, it's important to have functional components in the ensemble. Make sure each optimizer works decently for the problem before you leverage it as a node in the ensemble. Otherwise, you are going to be wasting your time and computational resources. Sometimes this would translate into a high monetary cost.

Moreover, make sure you leverage parallelism to optimize the ensemble's performance. This way, each optimizer will be working on a separate CPU thread or a different machine altogether, making the function of the ensemble much faster. If you are not familiar with parallelism, start with the *Distributed* package, which is part of the Base library of Julia (no need to install anything). You can read more about it here: https://docs.julialang.org/en/v1/stdlib/Distributed. Also, you can see an example of parallelism in action for an optimization ensemble in the book "AI for Data Science".

Additionally, it's good to remember that this whole ensemble business is a new area in the optimization field. It's much easier to use some off-the-shelf optimization library. This mindset, however, isn't all that creative and sometimes may not yield the desired results, even if it saves you time in the short-term.

Furthermore, although optimization is closely linked to AI, the latter is not a prerequisite for the former. You can be a great optimization professional without knowing the ins and outs of modern AI algorithms and systems. In fact, it's best if you study optimization independently since the lure of back-propagation and other similar algorithms used in ANNs is great, even if such algorithms aren't that great as optimizers for problems in different domains. Just like modern data models aren't tied to statistics, optimization methods don't depend on AI. It makes one wonder what else is possible if we apply optimization in other parts of data science.

Finally, heuristics may be great for optimization ensembles, but they are not the only option. So, if you have an optimizer or have a basic hybrid optimization system in place that works adequately for the problem at hand, you may want to stick with it, at least for the time being. There is no need to use a cannon to bring down a mosquito!

12.5 Summary

We examined optimization ensembles and how they are like ensembles of data models but a bit more esoteric. Nevertheless, they can be great tools for tackling particularly challenging problems or normal problems with better precision. We explored how parallelism is a useful and powerful strategy for optimization ensembles. We saw that the optimization ensembles run as long as any one node is active. Alternatively, you can add a terminating condition (heuristic) for each classifier so that it doesn't carry on its process when the improvement in the fitness function drops below a predefined threshold. We examined the role of heuristics in these ensembles and how they are essential, even if they are often relatively simple. Apart from the heuristic used for terminating the optimization process, there are others, such as the one for figuring out the output of the optimizer ensemble. Finally, we looked at some important considerations.

In the following few chapters, we'll look into how you can build new heuristics. We'll examine key characteristics of a heuristic and how you can turn an idea into something you can run on your computer through the Julia language.

PART IV

Designing and Implementing New Heuristics

While there have been terrific advances in the state of technology around heuristics, behavior blocking, and things like that, technology is only a part of the approach to solving the problem with the more important aspect involving putting the right process in place.

John W. Thompson

CHAPTER 13

Heuristic Objectives and Functionality

13.1 Overview of heuristic objectives and functionality

In heuristics, as in life, two things are of primary importance: where you are going and how you are getting there. In technical terms, these translate into the objectives and the functionality of the heuristic, a framework they often share with other data-based methods, including most data models. Of course, we don't just set out to create a heuristic and then think about what objectives it serves and how it functions (unless you are some heuristics genius). Heuristics are tools for creativity and every tool out there is engineered. Let's not forget that Leonardo da Vinci was an engineer and an artist (as well as a scientist and probably many other things), whose creativity stemmed from combining qualities on different sides of the spectrum.

Additionally, heuristics are there to serve a purpose, not just because they are fun. If we wanted to do fun stuff with math and programming, we'd be tackling various challenges on Project Euler or Code Abbey (a good idea to hone your problem-solving skills). Instead, we define the purpose of the heuristics by our objectives, which does not appear in documentation. The functionality of the heuristic stems from the objective and the means at our disposal. If you don't know a technical language well enough (i.e., mathematics and some decent programming language), the heuristic is just a nice idea to write about and inspire others.

When you ground an idea and make it into something that an engineer can understand and possibly implement, it becomes something else, just like the architect's design becomes a building that can offer shelter to others. To do this you need to get your hands dirty.

This chapter delves into the objectives of a heuristic, defining and understanding them, sometimes even breaking them down into simpler and more feasible objectives. Then it talks about the functionality of that heuristic and how we can meet these objectives practically. That's the most creative part of the whole process and the one that's the most challenging to many people. So naturally, it wouldn't make sense to talk about all that without at least saying a few words about the optimization aspect of objectives and functionality, something we'll cover next. This chapter concludes with some important considerations regarding heuristics objectives and functionality so that you gain a more holistic view of this topic. This chapter doesn't have a codebook accompanying it. Still, it's worth exploring some ideas for heuristics using paper and pen (or a whiteboard and a marker, if you prefer), to tackle them on a conceptual level.

13.2 Defining the objective(s) of a heuristic

Simon Sinek famously wrote "start with why" and gave numerous talks about this to all sorts of tech companies. Chances are that he was on to something because among the companies he consulted on various high-level matters, there were at least a couple of big tech ones. And as the famous German philosopher wrote, "he who has a strong enough 'why' can withstand any 'how'" (F. Nietzsche), it makes sense to conclude that knowing and being clear about the 'why' of something is very important, especially at the beginning of a project.

When I first started my work in pattern recognition (also known as *classification*) in the field of data analytics (data science wasn't a thing back then, though we did have computers, so it wasn't that long ago!), I wanted to be able to tell if certain data points were easy to classify or not. Taking it a step further, I wanted to know if the whole dataset or a subset of variables were easy to classify. That was the objective (or rather objectives) of the heuristic I developed, which came to be known as the index of discernibility (ID). Of course, I did more than that, but that was the impetus that drove the development of the corresponding scripts over the next few years (originally in Matlab and then Octave, before I migrated everything to R, Python, and Julia). Without having a properly defined objective and a supervisor who wasn't that keen on statistics, I would never have taken that direction in my PhD.

When it comes to research in machine learning, ideas only go so far—code must accompany the research. Ideas may have a place in more verbose fields like statistics, where theory plays a fundamental role, but not in hands-on areas with engineering as the mindset.

So, if you want to do some work with a new heuristic, you need to have a clear objective that serves a purpose. Even if some statistical method or metric does the same thing, the heuristics' data-driven approach makes them an alternative worth pursuing, especially if you aren't easily dismayed by programming. After all, the first version of your heuristic will probably be impractical (e.g., not scalable). Still, it's a step in the right direction. Looking back at the first version of the ID heuristic, I cannot help but cringe because of its inefficiency and limited scalability. Still, it paved the road for other versions that were more scalable and useful. So, if you are developing a new heuristic, try to think of the following to gauge its objectives:

1. What problem is it trying to solve, or at least help you with?
2. Could it be useful to other methods or systems?
3. What kind of data will it work with?
4. Has anyone done something similar that you need to reference?

At this point, don't concern yourself with what programming language you are going to use or what libraries in that language will come into play. Instead, first get a clear idea of what purpose this heuristic serves and then focus on the heuristic's functionality.

13.3 Working out the functionality of a heuristic

We need to make things so clear in our minds how a heuristic functions that someone who has never heard of our idea can take our specs and write a program (ideally in Julia) that will express this idea perfectly, meeting all of the heuristic's objectives. If everyone worked like this, there would be no need to troubleshoot anything that made it into production. Naturally, this would benefit data scientists since we wouldn't have to spend too much time fixing heuristics and models. Instead, we'd be working the data and communicating our findings as we are supposed to.

To work out the functionality of a heuristic, we need to design an algorithm that implements it efficiently and reliably. This may not be the only possible option, so creativity plays an important role in this endeavor. After all, anyone who understands algorithm design can put together an algorithm to implement some idea. Still, if that algorithm is of complexity $O(n^2)$ or something, you are better off without it! Also, if it requires a ton of data to work with, that's not a good sign either. The algorithm of a heuristic should be simple enough that any data professional could understand it and elegant enough that it can scale.

It is sometimes easier to be methodical about all this and try to implement the objectives one by one. For example, suppose there is a single objective to tackle. Then the heuristic is fundamental (simple and perhaps even ground-breaking) or the objective can be broken up into smaller objectives, which you need to tackle one by one. Note that just because we can implement a heuristic with a very simple algorithm doesn't mean that this is the best approach. This solution could be a local optimum in the solutions space containing all possible implementations of the heuristic. That's why, unlike data models, heuristics may be under constant scrutiny, constantly evolving. Those heuristics that remain stagnant are bound to become obsolete sooner or later.

So, if you are developing a new heuristic, try to answer the following questions, to work out its functionality:

1. Are the objectives as simple as possible?
2. How can objective A be implemented in the simplest way possible?
3. What assumption do we make by implementing the heuristic this way?
4. Can we implement the heuristic with no or few assumptions?
5. How can we extend the heuristic's functionality to cover other cases, such as higher dimensionality data?
6. If we had to apply this heuristic to a big data project, how would it scale?
7. Can the heuristic be parallelized?

It's important to note here that even if you don't answer all these questions, it's still better than not asking them at all. Knowing the heuristic's limitations is an asset that you can use to improve it afterward.

13.4 Optimizing the heuristic's objectives and functionality

Of course, we don't live in a perfect world, and no matter how hard we try, the chances are that the first version of our heuristic will need work. We often need to optimize the specs we discussed in the previous sections. Unfortunately, the optimization methods discussed won't help us much here. Still, at least we'll be comforted that even mathematically expressed problems tackled by a digital mind are hard to solve.

We shouldn't become complacent with the first draft of a heuristic (which is bound to be bad and possibly impractical). The aim of that first version is the proof of concept. As long as it yields results that make sense and pass all the unit tests we come up with (if we are more software engineering oriented), that's a success. After that, however, we need to make sure that it's relatively efficient and understandable. After all, if other people use it, they need to make sure it's worth their time and computational resources.

Optimizing the heuristic's objective involves ensuring the right scope and that it doesn't try to do too many things or just one very niche thing, which can be equally bad. The heuristic may pursue multiple objectives, but these can be extensions of one main objective. For example, the ID heuristic has a single objective (measuring how discernible/distinct the dataset's classes are) but extends that on a feature- and point-level. So, it doesn't just analyze the dataset as a whole (something a statistical test could easily do), but it offers some granularity that no other metric could offer.

Optimizing the heuristic's functionality involves ensuring it doesn't take forever to do its thing. For example, my PhD thesis showed a more efficient version of the ID heuristic. Since then, there have been others too, which are better and better, at least in terms of functionality. Sometimes just changing the language an algorithm is implemented in can make a big difference. Julia is 10x faster than Python, on average, and many more times faster than Matlab.

If statistics followed the same approach for improving its methods, all the stuff taught in universities and various data science courses would have been obsolete long ago. Instead, stats researchers are happy to add more methods and metrics to the corpus, since few dare to challenge the existing methods in any meaningful way. A heuristics-oriented researcher would have no inhibitions since he knows that heuristics are tools. The moment you start thinking that a heuristic cannot be improved any more is the time you should start thinking of restrictions to include in its documentation. That's one of the reasons why the "future work" section is there in various scientific research projects. No scientific theory is beyond falsification, a characteristic inherited by the various methods and metrics developed (engineered) scientifically, such as heuristics.

13.5 Important considerations

Let's now look at a few important considerations regarding this heuristic's objectives and functionality. First of all, no heuristic is great unless it has a clear objective and is well-implemented. What's more, if you haven't sorted out the objectives of a heuristic and optimized them to some extent, the chances are that its functionality will suffer too. So, it's best to be clear about what the heuristic is trying to do and focus on making it do just that. Heuristics attempt to make our problem-solving endeavors easier and possibly help us develop new and better ways to process data in a data-driven way.

Additionally, when it comes to complex heuristics that pursue a solution from various angles, it's best to explore the parallelism option. Even if the heuristic runs on a single computer, it can still apply multi-threading and yield better results in a given time frame. That's not a requirement for all heuristics, however. Sometimes, having a slick algorithm that has low complexity is enough.

Moreover, if you have a larger idea in mind that you want to implement in a heuristic, it may be better to use two or even three different heuristics. This will allow for better versatility, while a simpler heuristic will have more optimization potential than a larger one. Heuristics are not complete systems. For example, the UCA dimensionality reduction method I've developed (Uncorrelated Components Analysis) uses at least two different heuristics and yields better results than PCA. At the same time, it can guarantee linear and non-linear independence among the meta-features it constructs.

Finally, just like anything else in the heuristics world, the objectives and functionality of a heuristic are in a state of flux. So, it's good to take them as strong suggestions rather than absolute restrictions when developing new heuristics. They become more rigid at later stages of the heuristic development when creating documentation. The latter is also essential and enables others to appreciate the heuristic better and possibly improve it.

13.6 Summary

We looked at the objectives and functionalities of heuristics. The objectives are there to help us, and the user understands what the heuristic is supposed to do, while the functionality aims to make that happen efficiently. Additionally, defining the objectives first is essential since they can guide the whole development process. Without clear-cut objectives, the scope of a heuristic is vague, and its implementation is tricky, if not unfeasible. In addition, good functionality enables a heuristic to scale well and be an easy add-on to any data pipeline. We explored how optimizing both the objectives and the functionality of a heuristic are important and can often make the difference between a good heuristic and one that's never applied in real-world problems. Finally, we examined a few important considerations about heuristic development.

The next chapter will look into parameters, outputs, and usability for the first and simpler category of heuristics (metrics).

CHAPTER 14

Parameters, Outputs, and Usability for Metric Heuristics

14.1 Overview of parameters, outputs, and usability of metric heuristics

This chapter title sounds like a mouthful, but it is the next logical step from the previous chapter, as we now get more into the nitty-gritty of heuristics. After all, how can someone define the functionality of a heuristic? How would we apply this functionality when designing and implementing a new metric heuristic? We will answer these questions and explore how we can put together a methodology for making this process a workflow. There is no codebook for this chapter, but you can start putting together ideas and concepts on paper as you prepare for Chapter 16, where we'll take a hands-on perspective. I designed most of the heuristics over the past couple of years by sketching diagrams and formulas on my tablet and paper notebooks.

This chapter defines a heuristic's parameters and outputs and how they tie into the objectives and functionality aspects we covered previously. We'll then explore how we can figure out the heuristic's usability and scope. Next, we'll optimize the usability aspect and review some important considerations about this whole topic. Here we will focus exclusively on metric heuristics, and in the next chapter, we'll cover the more sophisticated method-related heuristics.

14.2 Defining a metric heuristic's parameters and outputs

Let's start our exploration of this topic by defining the parameters and outputs of the metric heuristic we plan to create. These are the IO-related data to the functions that will manifest the heuristic. We could also manifest the heuristics as classes if you are into this sort of programming. We'll start with the outputs since that's what matters the most to the end-user. These are usually one or more variables related to the heuristic's objectives. If the objectives are clear, the outputs definition should be straightforward. If you have that clear in your mind, you should be able to predict the type of variables involved and let Julia know to make it easier for whoever tests that function afterward. Although this is not necessary programmatically, it can save you time in the debugging stage.

Once you are clear about the outputs, even if you are not certain of their type, you can start looking at the inputs/parameters of the function. These are two-fold:

1. **Data-related**. These involve the data the heuristic will process. It can be scalar variables, vectors, matrices, or even tensors. All meaningful data qualifies as data-related inputs.

2. **Heuristic-related**. These have to do with the inner workings of the heuristic. For example, the parameter related to the distance metric used, any tolerance factor involved, and of course, anything related to efficiency optimizations. It is good practice to have some meaningful default values for all of these parameters to make the heuristic usage easier for the end-user and whoever wishes to go under the hood and possibly tweak it.

Equally important to all this is to create a short description of these parameters within the function's code. This can be inserted as a comment or even as a short blurb at the beginning of the function. In Julia, this is located right before the function is defined as a piece of multi-line text, within triple double-quotes, as in the example shown in Figure 14.1.

```
"""
    IsBinary(x)

Checks to see if a feature `x` is actually binary, even if it's coded as a Float,
and even if it's been normalized

"""
IsBinary(x::Array{Float64, 1}) = range(x) == 1 && length(unique(x)) == 2
```

Fig. 14.1 Example of blurb describing a function. This is a very useful feature of a well-developed heuristic.

In this simple example, it is quite straightforward what the output of the function IsBinary() is going to be. If, however, you needed to make it more explicit, you could add the "::Bool" part after the closing bracket of the function right before the first equals sign. Note that none of this is necessary for the function to run, since Julia isn't strict about types. However, having strongly-typed code allows for better transparency and disambiguation of the various functions that may share the same name, which is something fairly common in this programming language. Getting in the habit of writing code this way (at least in Julia) can save you lots of time in the long run, especially when the functions you create get more complex.

14.3 Figuring out a metric heuristic's usability and scope

Let's now continue our journey into creating this metric heuristic by looking at its usability and scope aspects. Let's start with the scope since that's closer to the perspective we're coming from when we look at the heuristic's objectives, although both usability and scope link to the heuristic's functionality. The objectives part we should always keep in mind since they drive the development of the heuristic. Otherwise, it's easy to get carried away and carry on sandboxing endlessly.

The heuristic's scope is the collection of its various use cases. This is reflected in its parameters and to some extent to its outputs, but it's also something more abstract. We need to know if the heuristic will apply to large datasets, such as lots of rows or columns. Many heuristics work perfectly for smaller datasets but don't manage to do much when the dimensionality gets higher. Although PCA is not technically a heuristic, it is a prime example. So, when developing a heuristic, we need to have that clear in our minds, optimizing it for the use cases it can and should handle. After that, we can always try to extend its scope by applying various optimizations and clever tweaks. However, when creating the heuristic, we need to focus on a relatively small and manageable scope, much like a startup would first focus on a minimum viable product (MVP) before developing its product line. A good example of scope that's not respected is the Pearson correlation metric, which isn't a heuristic since it's too attached to the plethora of assumptions of statistics metrics.

The heuristic's usability is closely linked to its scope. It has to do with the heuristic's usefulness and how it is perceived and utilized by the user. You may have the best heuristic in the world, but if you've neglected its usability, it's bound to remain unknown and perhaps even abandoned. That would be a waste of effort and time. That's why usability is very important when developing a heuristic, or any other program.

In practice, usability means clean code, such as proper indentation, intuitive variable names, meaningful comments, properly structured methods and functions, etc. A good (human-oriented) heuristic for this is imagining that you have no idea what the code you've written does and trying to make sense of it, something that happens organically if you were to not look at it for a long enough period. If you can follow the code relatively easily, that means the code is relatively clean. But, of course, there is always room for improvement.

Good documentation is also very important for the heuristic's usability and its scope. As we mentioned previously, writing a short blurb at the beginning of the corresponding function doesn't take much time. If the heuristic takes off and becomes accessible to a larger audience, ensure good documentation is available online, perhaps on a wiki-like web page or on a git-based repository like BitBucket. It doesn't matter where you host your code's documentation as long as it's well-written and contains examples to get newcomers started.

14.4 Optimizing a metric heuristic's usability

Since usability depends upon scalability and other aspects of its functionality, we need to know how it can be optimized. Besides, a metric heuristic (or any other heuristic) needs to make people's lives easier, especially when dealing with challenging problems for their work, such as quantifying a given phenomenon or gauging a variable.

A key strategy for optimizing the usability of a heuristic and its functionality is to develop a series of scenarios (use cases) to test the heuristic. This can be a benchmark dataset like the Wines Quality one we use in the code notebooks. Just ensure a variety of test use cases and try to break it to discover its limitations. This is similar to the unit-testing process that most software engineers are familiar with, though it goes a bit further since we also test for efficiency.

Additionally, you can beta-test the heuristic and see how others view it, especially those knowledgeable in data science or AI. Let them try to solve a problem using it and listen to their feedback. Perhaps it's good as a heuristic but doesn't scale very well. You can only improve it from that point onward if you leverage that information the beta-testers provide. Naturally, in some cases, it would be wise to have an NDA in place before the beta-testing process to ensure that your idea remains yours. Then again, this depends on the sophistication and commercial value of the heuristic at hand.

Furthermore, after the heuristic has been around for a while and you've forgotten the details of its implementation, you can build it anew. It sounds masochistic and wasteful, but this new approach to implementing the same idea may yield a different solution that's actually better. Perhaps the original implementation was the best you could do, but you may have evolved since then. If your new implementation isn't any better and you have evolved, maybe that's a solid implementation.

Finally, you can invite others to help you refine the heuristic and improve its usability. They may even give you some tips on how to improve its efficiency, or if they are adept and generous enough, they can make these improvements themselves. You can have up to five people on the free version of BitBucket, and you can always upgrade if you find that more people are willing to join your programming efforts on the heuristics front. You may even put the code on a public repository if you wish.

14.5 Important considerations

Since things aren't particularly cut-and-dry in heuristics, we must consider certain aspects of this topic of the heuristics' nitty-gritty before putting any of this into action. For instance, it's best to start with as few parameters (and outputs) as possible and build the equivalent of an MVP for the heuristic at hand. After that, you can always add more parameters to make it more versatile and functional. However, trying to do that from the beginning could make the whole process much more challenging.

What's more, it's always useful to have a couple of examples of how a metric heuristic works and how to leverage it in a typical problem. Extensive documentation can go a long way in making it more usable and useful.

Additionally, it's good to be transparent about the dependencies of the heuristic at hand. Once you start creating your own heuristics library, certain scripts will become commonplace and ubiquitous (you may find that the "include" command becomes second nature to you once you start putting together a new script). However, these additional scripts you'll be referencing need to be accessible to your new metrics, so make sure they are in the same folder or some parent/child folder in the new heuristic's folder structure.

Furthermore, as the programming language evolves, you need to ensure your script remains compatible with it. For metric heuristics, this is particularly important since they are bound to be part of other programs, which are going to break if the heuristic scripts don't work properly. So, be sure to test them as new language versions come about.

As far as scope is concerned, it's very important to know its limitations and write about them in the metric's documentation. Once you delve into heuristics, you'll realize that there is much more than meets the eye when measuring data and the relationships of variables than stats professionals assert. Perhaps statistics is there to teach us the limitations of a linear perspective and urge us to overcome them. One way to do that is by developing and using heuristics, particularly novel ones. After all, one of the lowest-hanging fruits of a clear understanding of the scope of something is to expand it whenever possible.

Finally, it's important to remember that when you develop a new metric heuristic, you do that to help the users solve certain kinds of data-related problems. It's not so that you can make a new publication or show off how clever and programmatically adept you are. The latter is bound to become apparent to those who can appreciate your work, sooner or later.

14.6 Summary

From a designer's perspective, we looked at the parameters, outputs, and usability of metric heuristics. Like any other heuristic, a metric heuristic needs to have clearly defined parameters (inputs), outputs, and usability (scope). We saw that defining the heuristic's outputs comes first, as it's closely linked to its objectives. Then, we can define its inputs, which are generally two-fold: data-related and heuristic-related. Data-related inputs involve the data that needs to be processed, while heuristic-related inputs involve the inner workings of the heuristic itself.

Additionally, we talked about a metric heuristic's usability and scope, which have to do with its functionality, though scope is also linked to its objectives. Usability has to do with how it is perceived and utilized by the end user. Scope involves the collection of use cases the heuristic can be applied. We looked at how a metric heuristic's usability can be optimized to make it even more accessible and useful to the end user. Finally, we examined some important considerations to have when it comes to metric heuristics.

Next, we'll look at method heuristics and how the whole parameters, outputs, and usability topic applies to them.

CHAPTER 15

Parameters, Outputs, and Usability for Method Heuristics

15.1 Overview of parameters, outputs, and usability of method heuristics

We will define the parameters and outputs of a method-related heuristic and then figure out its usability and scope. Next, we'll optimize the usability of such a heuristic since there is often room for improvement, especially when using a complex algorithm. Following that, we'll look at some important considerations regarding the parameters, the outputs, and the usability of method-related heuristics.

15.2 Defining a method heuristic's parameters and outputs

A method heuristic is more complex than a metric heuristic. It's not that a method heuristic requires more advanced data structures (although this could be the case). Instead, they have more moving parts and more things to tweak to fine-tune these algorithms. Also, the outputs are bound to be many-fold since these methods go into a lot of trouble calculating all sorts of variables.

Like in the case of a metric heuristic, it's a good idea to strong-type the inputs and perhaps even the outputs of the methods when coding them in Julia. Some Julia programmers would tell you that it's unnecessary and they may be right for most Julia scripts. However, if you use multiple dispatch (one of the key high-level characteristics of that programming language), it will make things so much easier if you have defined the types of your inputs and described each function. This way, you can tell it apart from other functions with the same name. Of course, to avoid all this trouble, you can always create new names for these variations of the original function. At least in this language, you have options like this, which is not the case for other high-level languages.

Some specialized parameters, like the distance metric for any distance-related process, can be included in the script after a semi-colon, making them optional. The drawback is that you'll have to type out the parameter's name so that Julia knows what input you are referencing when calling the corresponding function. So, if this seems too esoteric as a strategy, don't leverage it in your scripts. It's good to remember that you have this option for future iterations of this work, relating to newer versions of the heuristic.

Defining the outputs can also be more challenging if there are many of them. It's good practice to put the most important outputs first so that the user can isolate them more easily when using the heuristic script. It's also good to output variables that you are confident the user may use elsewhere when tackling the problem at hand. Otherwise, having too many outputs can be confusing and hurt the functionality of the heuristic.

15.3 Figuring out a method heuristic's usability and scope

Let's now continue our investigation of the method heuristic development by focusing on its usability and scope. The scope of the heuristic is important as it helps define what kind of scenarios the heuristic should tackle. It's easy to believe that it can handle more scenarios just because a method heuristic is more sophisticated than a metric one. Usually, this isn't the case, and it's important to be upfront about it when you design the heuristic.

An example of this is the hierarchical clustering algorithms, an excellent data-driven heuristic that develops groupings from the bottom up. It's hard not to get excited by them when reading about the theory of clustering and their ingenious approach. However, few people use them in practice since they don't scale very well, plus the K-means clustering heuristics (especially K-means++) are much faster and versatile, even if they can't yield the same result every time you run them. So, the scope of a hierarchical clustering method is limited, no matter how clever the algorithm that powers it.

The index of discernibility had a scope problem too. It has so many issues with scalability that the best way to fix them is to redesign the heuristic from scratch (which is what I did in a later version). So, the scope of a method heuristic is very important and perhaps something that's best assessed either by someone else knowledgeable about this topic or by you after you've moved on and don't feel too attached to your work.

As for the usability aspect of a method heuristic, it's similar to that of the metric heuristics. After all, testing a heuristic in various scenarios applies here, too, though the number of use cases is bound to be larger. Moreover, many method heuristics apply to both single- and multi-dimensional data. Also, just because the heuristic works well in the former case, it doesn't mean that it will work well, or even work at all, when the data involves multiple dimensions. So, putting all that in the documentation of the heuristic can greatly help with its usability.

Also, exploring the possibility of parallelism when implementing a method heuristic often makes sense and is worth looking into during the implementation phase of the heuristic. Since such a heuristic is more complex, it's bound to have some independent processes that can be parallelized either through multi-threading or through additional computers in a cluster array, for instance.

Finally, it would be meaningful to create extensive documentation for more sophisticated method heuristics. Perhaps an article containing a couple of examples can make things more understandable to the end user and enhance the heuristic's usability.

15.4 Optimizing a method heuristic's usability

Naturally, a method heuristic's usability also needs some optimization. However, it's a bit more elaborate a process than the optimization of a metric heuristic's usability. Besides, a method heuristic aims to make people's lives easier, especially when other alternatives fail or are inapplicable. So why not try to make things even easier for them through optimized usability in the method heuristics we develop?

In general, just like in the metric heuristics, it's good to start small and build up from there when developing a method heuristic. Perhaps, in the beginning, work with some predefined values (constants) in your method. Later on, you can make the methods more flexible by using a parameter in the place of each one of these constants. The constants themselves can still linger in the script, but their use may differ. It may seem like overkill to have a lot of parameters for a simple method, but some methods may require it to be more usable. After all, the dynamics change quite a bit when dealing with multi-dimensional space. That's why it's sometimes useful to allow for different distance metrics rather than the Euclidean or Manhattan (city-block) distances, which aren't all that great in high dimensionalities. The same goes for other things, like densities and geometrical shapes. Especially spheres, which are notoriously peculiar in high-dimensional space.

Additionally, like with metric heuristics, beta-testing is very useful for exploring a method heuristic's usability and extending it. The difference here is that this testing needs to be more extensive since it's a more sophisticated tool. Besides, performance is also a factor since different kinds of data may make the heuristic perform slower or not work. In addition, pesky NaNs may appear, indicating that a certain niche scenario hasn't been properly addressed. Naturally, you can't have these kinds of issues if you want the heuristic to be useful to many people, most of whom may not be willing or capable of tweaking your script to make sure it works.

Another good optimization strategy for a method heuristic is to branch it out with various versions of it, specializing in specific data types. The multiple dispatch feature of Julia can be a useful asset in that. Of course, all this may limit the heuristic's scope, but that's not necessarily the case. You just employ a series of specialized functions to tackle the niche use cases one by one, much like an optimization ensemble does in its domain. The end user isn't going to care how the result comes about, plus the Julia community is quite fond of the multiple dispatch approach in scripts of that language. It's a more creative application of the "divide and conquer" strategy that's so popular in programming.

What's more, you can explore specialized packages to see if you can optimize certain processes of your heuristic's algorithm. For example, I've been computing the neighborhood of a data point using a distance matrix and the nearest neighbor algorithm, which seriously lacks in performance. There was nothing wrong with this strategy or its implementation. It was just very inefficient. Unfortunately, since I mainly dealt with people who didn't know any better either, I became complacent and thought I was working with the state-of-the-art. Fortunately, I discovered K-dimensional trees one day and learned that a Julia developer had developed a package, so I didn't need to develop my own. So, I started using that package from that point onward for all my neighborhood-related scripts (in the next chapter, you'll have a chance to have some hands-on experience with one such script). Bottom line, sometimes being open to the possibility of a better way of dealing with a process efficiently can go a long way in optimizing the method heuristics that rely on that process.

A final optimization strategy for this type of heuristic is mentoring. Not just being mentored by someone more knowledgeable about these topics, but also mentoring others yourself. Sometimes when trying to explain something, you learn it better and go into depths that you didn't consider beforehand. Of course, when you are on the receiving end of a mentoring relationship, the benefit is more accessible. It's best to focus on mentors who have some experience and value their time enough to charge for it. There are very few things in this world that are free of charge regarding knowledge and know-how.

15.5 Important considerations

Let's now look at some important considerations for the parameters, outputs, and usability of this category of heuristics. For starters, it's good to leverage different datasets, especially datasets that have a semblance to the real world, when testing your heuristics. Otherwise, you'll end up with something that works well with synthetic (typically, random) data and nothing else. Also, real-world scenarios may have peculiarities worth exploring since these niche cases may break the heuristic. After all, the latter needs to work with any data given, not just data that follows a particular distribution.

Additionally, it's good to be clear and knowledgeable about the problem the method heuristic is trying to solve. A good understanding of the challenges involved can help you design it well and, equally importantly, present it in a way that will help the users derive value from it. This attitude reflects how you define the parameters and outputs of the heuristic. Heuristics are fun to create and optimize, but they are not an end!

Some heuristics work together with other heuristics as part of a library. It's good to figure that out early on so that you design their outputs accordingly. The same goes for other aspects of the heuristics, such as their scope. Having designed such libraries of heuristics, I can attest that it's a big project to create such a collection of interlinked and interdependent functions expressing all sorts of heuristic ideas. So, before embarking on such a journey, make sure you've mastered independent (stand-alone) method heuristics first.

Method heuristics can get complicated quickly since they are more like medium-sized functions than short-sized metric heuristics. So, it's good to remember that less is more and that keeping these medium-sized functions slim can save us a lot of problems later on. At the same time, the users will more likely use the heuristics if it is an easy-to-understand script rather than the equivalent of a novel in terms of complexity.

Finally, sometimes you have too much functionality packed in a single method heuristic, something the KISS rule will alert you when trying to apply it. It would make sense to break up the heuristic into two or more functions (sub-heuristics?) and work with those. This can give rise to a whole script of heuristics, which is often the case when developing something new. This doesn't have to be a library, but it may grow to become one eventually. It's also a good practice to separate the auxiliary functions used in this work from the main methods, to make the code in that script easier to understand and maintain.

15.6 Summary

We covered the parameters, outputs, and usability of a method heuristic and how all the different aspects of a heuristic come together to express its objectives and functionality. We looked at how the parameters of a method heuristic can make it more flexible and help its usability. Also, how outputs play a similar role, though including too many may have the opposite effect. Additionally, we looked at how usability and scope factor in when it comes to this sort of heuristic. Furthermore, we saw how method heuristics could optimize parameters, outputs, etc. Including some advanced package, for example, can go a long way in improving a heuristic's efficiency and make it more scalable than you may have thought possible. Finally, we examined some important considerations to have regarding this topic.

Next, we'll roll up our sleeves and apply what we've theorized in these past three chapters. We'll focus on two heuristics, one metric- and one method-related. Naturally, this is just the beginning of our heuristics development journey since you can go about creating your own heuristics afterward.

CHAPTER 16

Developing and Optimizing a Heuristic

16.1 Process overview for developing a new heuristic

At this point, you know how we can put together a heuristic based on an idea. We have covered the theoretical, which is a necessary prerequisite before we start working on a computer to implement this idea. As Abraham Lincoln once said, "Give me six hours to chop down a tree and I will spend the first four sharpening the ax." Hopefully, you've sharpened your metaphorical ax in the past three chapters, and now you can now put it to work!

We'll look into two specific examples of heuristic ideas, one for a metric and another for a method. We'll move from conceptual to practical (implementation as programming scripts). We'll also examine important considerations regarding new heuristics. A codebook accompanies this chapter, but it's best not to look at it before reading the whole chapter and then trying out some things on your own. In the meantime, recall the various aspects of a heuristic in Figure 16.1.

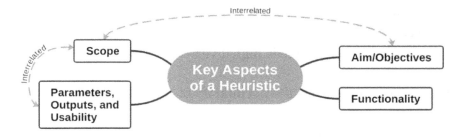

Fig. 16.1 Key aspects of a heuristic and their relationships.

16.2 Defining the objectives and functionality of the new heuristic

16.2.1 Overview

As we move from drawing board to Julia code development to testing, we'll look into a heuristic to measure diversity and another to measure the peculiarity of dataset points. I discussed the first one in a 2019 blog. As for the index of peculiarity heuristic, this is something I came up with while writing this book. Both heuristics must scale well. Otherwise, their usability would be limited.

16.2.2 A heuristic to measure diversity in a variable

So, we have a continuous variable and we're curious about how diverse its data. Not how spread out, mind you, but how diverse. Measures of spread like the standard deviation can measure, well, spread, and they do so quite well. But this assumes there is a center point for comparison. Also, measures of spread tend to take any positive values (or, in some extreme cases, the value of zero). Wouldn't it be great to have a measure that didn't care about the center point and took values between 0 and 1, inclusive? In a nutshell, that's what this heuristic will do.

How will it do that? Well, in a scalable way, for sure, so it cannot have too many calculations. Also, it needs to be able to pinpoint extreme cases and take them into account. This can help normalize its outputs to always be between 0 and 1. Naturally, if a heuristic like this will manifest, it cannot be perfect, so we need to prepare for cases where it fails. Before you read the rest of the chapter, can you think of a scenario where the diversity heuristic will yield an irrelevant result (i.e., a very low value when there is high diversity or vice versa)?

16.2.3 A heuristic to measure the peculiarity of dataset points

I have to admit, such an idea for a heuristic sounds peculiar, if not out of place. However, remember the index of discernibility? That heuristic has shown again and again to be very useful, and it relies on a similar idea. The key difference though is that ID requires a target variable and that variable needs to be discrete (i.e., it works with datasets tackled with the classification methodology). What if we could manage a similar kind of dataset assessment but without a target variable? This could be useful for all kinds of problems, plus it might help us understand how "interesting" the dataset is. Much like the diversity heuristic but on a higher dimensionality, a heuristic that measures peculiarity could help gauge the data's deviation from what's expected (i.e., what's easily predictable). If this reminds you of the chi-square test, it should. However, unlike that elegant statistical method, the heuristic we are examining here doesn't rely on the chi-square distribution or any other distribution. Also, this heuristic applies to continuous variables, which you may want to normalize first, for reasons that will become apparent later on.

But how would this index of peculiarity method deliver? It could examine particular neighborhoods of the dataset, perhaps the neighborhood of each data point (let's call it x), and see if something is off in that part of the dataset. Of course, we need to define what we mean by "off". So, we can perhaps find the center of that neighborhood, a fairly straightforward operation. Then we can calculate the distance of that center point from the actual center of the neighborhood (x). Handy as they are, distances tend to be all over the place, so we may want to normalize it somehow. The radius (r) of the neighborhood can be a good normalizing factor since there is no way that the new center point will be beyond the neighborhood, so its distance has to be between 0 and r.

16.2.4 The value question

All this may be nice and dandy, but we still haven't answered the paramount question of "So what?" After all, why should we bother with these heuristics in the first place and not use some measure of spread and some kernel density method? The answer to this involves the underlying idea behind both of these heuristics (and many other heuristics based on the same philosophy). This is the notion of decentralization. This is crucial in the dataset domain, where we tend to spend most of our time as data professionals in charge of advanced analytics tasks. After all, there is no reason that a single data point (such as average) is more important than everything else.

Moreover, why should we let a whole variable revolve around a shaky single data point when assessing it? And if we cannot make sense analyzing a single variable based on that single centrality value, why should a collection of variables (i.e., a dataset) revolve around a single data point?

16.2.5 Your part

Everything seems fine in theory, but how can you put all this into code? That's where you come in. You can start working on these ideas at any point in this chapter, maybe even now. Then, you can see the suggested solution and get some ideas to improve your work. The code in the Neptune codebook of this chapter is just my approach to these heuristics. There may be better implementations of these ideas that are still waiting to be discovered and implemented.

16.3 Defining the parameters, outputs, and usability of the new heuristics

Let's now look at the new heuristics' parameters, outputs, and usability. Note that this is just one possible implementation of the ideas presented previously. In fact, it's best to be skeptical about anything heuristics-related since these metrics and methods are work-in-progress. So, if you can come up with a better implementation of these heuristics ideas, please let me know what you come up with. We can all learn from each other.

16.3.1 Parameters, outputs, and usability of the diversity heuristic

Since the diversity heuristic is a metric heuristic, it is the simpler of the two examined in this chapter. It involves taking a single variable x of a given length n, calculating all the distances of all consecutive points, and figuring out how they compare with the maximum possible distance. The latter can be calculated as follows: $d_{max} = (x_{max} - x_{min}) / (n - 1)$. How do we leverage this exactly? We can take the difference of the median of differences and the maximum difference (d_{max}), divide it by d_{max} and subtract it from one. Naturally, what comes out of all this is a single float number, which is the output of the heuristic.

As for its usability, diversity is quite scalable and easy to use. We can use it without any programming skill or even theoretical knowledge like any other well-defined metric. It spits out a number between 0 and 1 (inclusive), with higher numbers denoting more diversity in the data.

One fairly evident use case is more balanced sampling (optimizing diversity scores across the various variables of the data). Also, it can be applied to the evaluation of synthetic datasets, to ensure congruency with the original data. However, other applications of the diversity heuristic remain to be discovered.

16.3.2 Parameters, outputs, and usability of the index of peculiarity heuristic

The index of peculiarity heuristic is more complex because it's a method heuristic applicable to multi-dimensional data. It involves two main tasks:

1. figuring out how peculiar a given data point x is in relation to a given dataset X, and

2. figuring out how peculiar each one of the points of a given dataset X are, in relation to the rest of the dataset.

In both cases, these data structures are the inputs of the corresponding functions. In the second case, however, an additional parameter comes into play. This relates to a check for whether the variables are normalized or not. After all, if we were to run this function again and again, there is no point in checking every time. Best to normalize the data beforehand and then let the heuristic do its thing without worrying about this matter. In any case, it's good to be aware of this detail, since normalized data is crucial for a smoother calculation of distances.

The outputs of these two functions involve two things: the IP score(s) and the center point(s) of the neighborhood(s) involved. For the second function, the method yields an additional output, the median of all the IP scores, to understand how peculiar the dataset is overall.

As for usability, this function is quite self-explanatory. It uses K-D trees on the backend to scale well. High IP scores mean that the data is quite sparse and possibly diverse (a bit like the diversity metric but not exactly the same), while low IP scores mean that the data is more or less predictable. This EDA-related application is the only viable one found so far, though some experiments regarding data summarization using this heuristic have taken place too with marginal success.

16.3.3 Scope matters for the two heuristics

Both heuristics have a next to impossible scope to deduce by looking at their inputs and outputs. After all, if the corresponding functions compile, everything should be fine, right? Julia might give you the green light, but the real world is a stricter judge and is bound to have higher standards.

For the diversity heuristic, the scope (for this version at least) involves small datasets or datasets with many different values. If at least half of the values in the variables examined are not unique, the diversity heuristic will yield a value of 0. (Can you figure out why this is?) So, either you take a summary or sample of the data before applying diversity, or don't use this heuristic.

As for the IP heuristic, its scope is much broader. However, it is limited to matrices, so it's not supposed to work with vectors. Nevertheless, there is a walk-around that you can apply (see codebook for details), but it's not always a good idea. Even if Julia can see a vector as a matrix and process it using the IP method, the result may not be as useful. After all, the heuristic was designed with geometry in mind, so using it with single-dimensional data is going too far.

However, the scope is not set in stone. You can extend it with the right tweaks and make both of these heuristics more useful. So what are you going to sacrifice in the process, and is the sacrifice worth it? That's a question you may often have to ask yourself whenever you look into expanding the scope of a heuristic.

16.4 Important considerations

Things will most likely not go according to plan. Even a clear idea about the heuristic may not translate into a good piece of code for that heuristic you envisioned. So, manage your expectations accordingly. For every heuristic that I have successfully implemented, at least two others didn't make it, even if I based them on the same idea as the one that made it. You can't know in advance if a good idea will manifest well, while perseverance and creativity are always essential when building new heuristics. What's more, just because a heuristic is useful and scalable, it doesn't mean it should remain stagnant. There is often additional potential in the heuristic that you may want to explore by refining the whole thing further.

Additionally, when building a new heuristic, always make sure that someone else tests it after it's complete. Otherwise, you may never finish this project if they start pitching ideas and enhancements. It takes a special kind of person to give you feedback that can help you build it better, and not everyone who pretends to be such a person is indeed qualified and capable. Good mentors are hard to find, especially in the data-driven field.

Furthermore, a new heuristic is judged differently from something that's been around for a while. If you come up with a new performance metric for ML models, its issues are bound to be overseen, at least in the beginning, because it needs to be tested thoroughly. Perhaps it's great for a certain niche of use cases involving a certain type of model.

Finally, your creativity will evolve, just like every ability you have. So, if it doesn't yield the best fruits yet, don't give up. Instead, cultivate that skill over the years by first appreciating good heuristics and understanding how they work.

16.5 Summary

We explored how a new heuristic comes about, starting from its objectives and functionality and drilling into its more detailed aspects, such as its parameters, outputs, and usability. We also talked a bit about its scope. We looked at the diversity and index of peculiarity heuristics, how they measure how diverse a given variable is, and the peculiarity of data points in a dataset (multi-dimensional data). They apply to any data that is continuous. Additionally, we saw that these heuristics are manifestations of the same core idea of decentralization applied to data. Although they take a stab at it from entirely different angles, they aim to measure something about the data without using any central point (e.g., the mean) like most other measures and methods do to assess the data. Moreover, we looked at these heuristics' parameters, outputs, and usability and how to apply them for EDA and possibly other applications. Finally, we examined some important considerations when dealing with a new heuristic.

We'll look at various supplementary topics regarding heuristics in the few chapters. The idea is to better understand the whole subject from a holistic perspective and balance the enthusiasm you may have about them with down-to-earth views.

PART V

Supplementary Topics on Heuristics

Heuristics are simplified rules of thumb that make things simple and easy to implement. But their main advantage is that the user knows that they are not perfect, just expedient, and is therefore less fooled by their powers. They become dangerous when we forget that.

Anonymous

CHAPTER 17

Heuristics' Limitations

17.1 Overview of heuristic limitations in general

Heuristics can be enticing and even dangerous when we trust them too much and forget that they are imperfect. Perhaps that's why most data science and AI professionals opt for more established tools, which compromise their creativity. It's not easy to balance leveraging heuristics as ways to express and nourish creativity, all while relying on other tools for cases when heuristics fail to deliver. In essence, it's a matter of discerning when to use them and to what extent. This whole matter becomes significantly easier when we consider their limitations in our decision process.

Throughout the book, we mentioned the limitations of specific heuristics. After all, each heuristic is a relatively unique algorithm, so it has its own set of limitations. However, heuristics tend to have some inherent limitations that we will explore here to avoid pitfalls.

So, in this chapter, we'll look at the limitations of heuristics in their capability to generalize. After all, they are not robust models, just tools to help us out with data modeling work in analytics. We'll also look at limitations of heuristics in terms of accuracy and end with some important considerations.

17.2 Limitations in generalization capability

Let's start our exploration of the limitations of heuristics by looking at their generalization capability. Few can argue about the importance of generalization. After all, if we can generalize a result or insight based on our data analysis, this makes it robust and generally more useful. Since heuristics are useful, shouldn't they generalize well too?

Yes in a perfect world but no in reality. After all, they are tools, not models. Models are complex enough and they are developed in very challenging conditions so that they have good generalization. That's their main job. On the other hand, heuristics help us understand the data better, tweak it a bit, find good solutions to a problem and analyze the data creatively. They are not there to substitute models, and as a result, they don't always generalize well.

Specifically, for data-related heuristics, they may not be able to reflect the whole dataset because they focus mostly on individual data points, resulting in mediocre generalization. Or perhaps they rely a lot on methods that do not scale well, like the vast majority of distance metrics. They aim to give us an idea of what the data is like without thinking about scalability and generalization. Someone could argue that almost all descriptive statistics do the same, so we should not rely on them too much. This is why plots are so popular in data science work.

As for optimization-related heuristics, they may not generalize well because of the nature of the problems involved. For example, a particular optimization heuristic may be great at solving the current problem, but it may not be able to do the same for all kinds of problems of that family. Maybe it needs some tweaking in its parameters or even its functionality. That's why it's challenging to find a one-size-fits-all solution to the various optimization problems we encounter and why many metaheuristics are involved. Also, that's why we may seek to use an ensemble of optimizers to tackle a larger collection of such problems.

We could theoretically make a heuristic more generalizable, but the more we succeed in this, the more complex and, therefore, cumbersome the heuristic becomes. We'll talk more about this matter later on in this chapter.

17.3 Limitations in accuracy

Limitations in accuracy are a key shortcoming of heuristics, especially when complex data is involved. This includes all optimization where we look for an accurate solution to a problem. However, in both cases, the accuracy a heuristic yields isn't as great as we'd like, especially if we are coming from a non-heuristic place where we are used to established models and deterministic algorithms.

Data-related heuristics may give us a good idea of certain trends and patterns in the dataset, but they aren't 100%, especially when its dimensionality is high. However, we expect this because of the distance metrics they use. Also, heuristics were designed to provide insights and help us better organize the data, not predict something accurately. So, in a way, it's not heuristics that are at fault but rather our expectations. For example, the median density of a dataset as calculated by the corresponding heuristic may not match the density of that dataset calculated more accurately using a convex hull to find its volume. Still, it's a good enough approximation, plus we usually care about the relative differences among the densities of the various data points anyway.

Optimization-related heuristics have a bigger problem with accuracy. They specialize at being efficient and providing a good-enough solution rather than yielding the best possible solution. So, if we expect them to provide the absolute best solution to a given problem, we will be disappointed. What's more, highly complex search spaces with an objective function whose values don't vary much, may fail to yield a good solution, as it's possible to get trapped in a local optimum. This is particularly the case when there are lots of dimensions involved. Still, we can overcome this problem by running the optimizer again with a different starting point or a different set of parameters. Alternatively, we can use different optimization algorithms and compare the results.

17.4 Why these limitations exist and trade-offs

But why are there limitations like these in heuristics? Couldn't we just design heuristics better so they don't have these limitations? Answering this question is the first step to understanding heuristics deeper.

Although it is possible to make a heuristic quite robust and accurate, this usually comes at the loss of something else, such as scope. For example, one of the first variants of the index of discernibility, the distance-based index of discernibility (DID), can predict how good any given feature is for all sorts of datasets. Yet as a heuristic, it's more limited than the original discernibility metrics, since it cannot predict the discernibility of an individual data point. It relies a lot on various distances but doesn't use the hypersphere approach, and as a result, it's more of a high-level heuristic.

We observe a similar phenomenon in optimization-related heuristics that are quite accurate in certain problems. For example, I've developed a heuristics-based optimizer that relies on variables constrained at a very specific interval (between 0 and 1, inclusive), while also relatively few in number. This optimizer may work better (i.e., is more accurate) than other optimization algorithms for this set of problems, but it's not as versatile.

Hopefully, it's becoming clear that the more generalized or accurate a heuristic is, the more specialized it is. So, there is a trade-off between usefulness and generalization capability or accuracy. Although this trade-off isn't as obvious in certain heuristics, it's an underlying pattern that describes most of them—a heuristic of sorts about heuristics!

17.5 Important considerations

What about limitations of heuristics in general, and how this can be a limiting factor in how we use them? Namely, what do we need to keep in mind to make the most of heuristics despite their various limitations?

First of all, we can learn a large variety of heuristics so that we use the less limited ones for each problem we tackle. Just because a few are more popular, it doesn't mean that we should use just those. The larger the toolbox of heuristics we have at our disposal, the better equipped we'll be to tackle our data problems without being too limited by this or the other heuristics.

Additionally, we shouldn't be too afraid to tweak the heuristics, if necessary. This way, we can address their limitations and patch them to the extent possible. We'll probably need to write some extra code for this, but it's an investment since we're upgrading our tools and refining our programming skills. As a side-product, we are honing our creativity and enhancing our problem-solving abilities.

Moreover, we can also develop our own heuristics whenever all other heuristics are unable to help. We saw that it's not a daunting task, even if it's more challenging than merely modifying an existing heuristic. Still, it's a good opportunity to dig into the data deeper and understand it better, using the new heuristic as a vehicle of sorts in this exploratory journey.

Finally, if we cannot do any of that, we can always develop different ways to tackle the problem. Perhaps a conventional tool can help us out, or we can rely on some data model or other established algorithm. Heuristics are there to help, but we should be open to using other tools whenever heuristics fail to provide an adequate solution.

17.6 Summary

We looked at the limitations of heuristics from various angles. First, we saw that it's inevitable for heuristics to fail at generalization or accuracy, at least for certain complex problems. This is due to their nature and is a side-effect of their versatility and efficiency in the problems they can help us tackle. If heuristics were more specialized (and therefore have a more limited scope), they'd have more generalization capabilities and higher accuracy, but they'd also be less versatile tools. We also looked at several examples where the generalization capability and the accuracy of a heuristic are limiting. We examined the hidden trade-off between a heuristic's usefulness (expressed as versatility) and its generalization/accuracy potential. Finally, we looked at a few useful considerations about the limitations of heuristics.

With limitations aside, in the next chapter, we will focus on the potential of heuristics.

CHAPTER 18

Heuristics' Potential

18.1 Overview of heuristics' potential in general

There is a reason why heuristics is an active area of research and has been quite promising over the years, especially in areas like machine learning and AI, where the data-driven approach dominates. Heuristics could potentially transform the way we work with data, from exploratory data analysis, to optimization, auxiliary processes, and even model-building. The latter is particularly the case for machine learning models, which are also state-of-the-art, especially in predictive analytics. In this chapter, we'll look at all of these facets of the topic, highlighting how you could contribute to expanding this domain, making data science more data-driven and decentralized.

18.2 Heuristics' potential for EDA

EDA tools are limited and often capture only certain aspects of the data. We saw how some heuristics could help shed light on this matter by analyzing the relationships among the various variables, especially when a target variable is involved. But there is so much more to it than that, since many tasks that are part of EDA are often neglected, leading to a heavier feature engineering stage following EDA. For example, what if there were ways to pinpoint outliers using heuristics automatically? Conventional methods are crude and relatively subjective, requiring thresholds for figuring out whether a point is an outlier or not. Alternatively, some specialized support vector machine (SVM) model is used, when more than one dimensions are present. A heuristic designed for this task could handle this problem much more eloquently and efficiently.

We can tackle inliers with a similar heuristics-based approach. So far, few people bother with them, but they can be an issue in certain scenarios since they don't add any value to the dataset. In a way, they are noise, much like most outliers, though not everyone knows how to deal with them properly. However, you don't need to be an expert to know that removing noisy data points, such as inliers, can make data science tasks much easier, especially whenever clustering is required.

Additionally, we could have heuristics to handle the relationships of specialized variables, like ordinal ones. These variables are quite common in the data involved in surveys, which seems to be growing over the past few years. Also, knowing how to handle such variables may lead to developing such features in the future for a variety of problems, such as NLP.

Finally, using heuristics, we could examine new ways to measure centrality and spread in a continuous variable. This way, we can have a more reliable view of the data, not influenced by abnormalities in the distribution it follows. Heuristics of this category could be linked to some of the ones dealing with different EDA tasks since many of these tasks are interlinked on a deeper level. Since finding links among seemingly unrelated things is a characteristic of creativity, this kind of work can be creative.

EDA is a creative process, and leveraging heuristics here makes good sense. It's up to the innovative and eager to view it this way and explore what other heuristics could be discovered in this exploration of the various datascapes.

18.3 Heuristics' potential for optimization

Optimization is an area where heuristics are blooming and will probably continue doing so in the foreseeable future. It's no wonder that most books on heuristics focus on metaheuristics for optimization applications. Besides, these are the most complex problems you would encounter, and sometimes solving them efficiently is the greatest value-add for an organization. These problems are very general in their applicability, making them even more appealing since they can fit in all kinds of domains.

Optimization-oriented heuristics still have a role to play, as for example, in the case of a problem involving certain restrictions. We can tackle these problems with advanced metaheuristics that efficiently consider these restrictions. For example, through the introduction of a "penalty" to the fitness score, whenever a restriction is violated. When we have parameters in a specific range (between zero and 1), the optimization space is much better defined and conventional optimization methods, although applicable, may not be the most efficient way to go. Also, sometimes the restrictions are such that we only need to optimize a smaller set of variables. For instance, if we are trying to find the weights for something, which tends to add up to 1, we don't need to optimize all of them since the last weight is just 1 minus the sum of the other weights. This can simplify the problem, making the whole process more efficient.

We can also use heuristics for optimizing complex problems through a combination of optimization algorithms. This may seem excessive, but an adaptive strategy can make a big difference if you deal with challenging search spaces. For such a strategy to work, we may need to have two or more optimizers at play, sometimes one of them managing the other optimizers. As we saw in the optimization ensembles chapter, this complex situation can be simplified using heuristics.

Finally, since some domain-specific problems incorporate specialized knowledge, there can be specialized optimizers to tackle them more efficiently. Perhaps these can be found by tweaks to the existing optimization methods, using some heuristics that embody this domain knowledge somehow. If you are up for a challenge, that's a possibility worth exploring.

Optimization is a somewhat creative process, particularly when complex problems are involved. So, leveraging heuristics in this scenario can also make good sense. It's up to the most inventive among us to approach them this way and explore what other (meta)heuristics could be discovered.

18.4 Heuristics' potential for auxiliary processes

Auxiliary processes may not be in the limelight since they don't directly link to a value-add in data science work. Still, they are useful in the niche cases they aim to cover. These cases can fit in various parts of the pipeline and provide value in all kinds of data science projects.

An example of such a heuristic is the data summarization one, which involves selecting data points for a given variable in a deterministic manner to best represent the data overall. However, this process is not the same as sampling, which is almost always random. Data summarization figures out the most important points for a given variable and provides their indexes, or in some cases, yields a mathematical approximation of the most representative points. The latter option is quite useful when the dataset is small. In any case, the data summarization heuristic manages to maintain the key characteristics of the data, even if it generally yields a high compression ratio. The best part of this heuristic is that it doesn't require many parameters from the user, and it figures out how to best summarize the data based on the variable at play. Performing data summarization on the target variable in a regression problem can be very useful as it can also help us figure out which data points to use in the feature set. Alternatively, we can also perform data summarization on specific features for EDA purposes. Note that summarized data may not be homogeneous in terms of importance, as certain data points in the summary may carry more weight than others.

Another interesting multi-purpose heuristic for all kinds of auxiliary processes is that of finding the optimal bin width for a single variable, as is the case of a histogram. This is one of the simplest heuristics out there and is known as the Freedman-Diaconis rule:

$$h=2\times\text{IQR}\times n^{-(1/3)}$$

where IQR is the inter-quantile range (Q3 – Q1) that's often used in box plots, and n is the total number of data points. The value h can help us find the best number of bins *b* for a histogram, which is b = [(max – min) / h], where max and min are the maximum and minimum values of the variable and [.] is the rounding operator to the nearest integer. Also, once we calculate the number of bins, it's wise to redefine *h* based on it, using the formula h = (max – min) / b. This way, the variable will be evenly divided into *b* bins, each one of size *h*.

We can use this heuristic for various applications involving binning, not just for histograms. Also, we can enhance it by using more accurate ways to compute the internal range (in this case IQR), so that it's more inclusive of different distributions of data, such as multi-modal or highly skewed ones.

18.5 Heuristics' potential for model-building

Heuristics have a long way to go when it comes to model-building, even if they have been used there successfully and data models are a big value-add for many organizations. So here we'll look at only a couple of examples.

First of all, the decision tree model tackles classification and regression problems. This model is often referred to as CART, which stands for Classification And Regression Tree. The CART classification uses a heuristic called the Gini index, which in regression problems uses variance or some other heuristic that is applicable for continuous variables. We apply both of these metrics on each feature *x* used in the tree, taking the form of a node. The idea is that by minimizing the gini index or the variance, we can figure out how to best split the feature *x* so that the outcome of that node is as good as possible, making the overall outcome of the decision tree more accurate.

Gini index is a heuristic for measuring impurity, be it for a given feature or all the features of the tree, in respect to the target variable *y*. So, for a given set of features X we can calculate the gini index as follows:

$$Gini(X) = 1 - \Sigma p_i^2 \text{ for } i = 1 \text{ to nf}$$

where p_i is the overlap proportion of the feature X_i with the target variable y (i.e., the similarity of the binary version of X_i and y), and nf is the number of features.

When it comes to a given feature X_i, the gini index is calculated as follows:

$$Gini(X_i) = w_1 * Gini(X_i = true) + w_2 * Gini(X_i = false)$$

where w_1 and w_2 are the proportions of the cases of X_i being true and X_i being false, respectively, in the whole dataset.

It's good to reiterate that if X_i is not a binary variable, we need to make it binary using a threshold, above which it takes the value 1 (true) and below which it takes the value 0 (false). This binarization process takes place in every tree whenever continuous variables are involved. This is why when using CART, we don't need to normalize the dataset.

Another heuristic applied in model-building is K-means++, a modern clustering algorithm. Like K-means, it uses a couple of heuristics, Dunn index and silhouette width (or silhouette analysis as it's often called), for figuring out the best cluster structure. After figuring out the best points to use as centroids (cluster centers), K-means takes it a step further by figuring out a good strategy for assigning the initial centroids (the original K-means algorithm assigns them randomly). This is done through another heuristic, namely the distance to the farthest centroid, d_i, calculated through the following formula:

$$d_i = \max_{(j:1 \to m)}\|x_i - C_j\|^2$$

where x_i is a point in the dataset whose distance to the centroids we calculate, C_j is the j-th centroid, and m is the number of centroids already discovered. In other words, once a bunch of centroids are picked, we get the next one by finding a point that's as far as possible from them. The first centroid is picked at random. So, the algorithm itself is still stochastic, but also deterministic once the first centroid is selected.

Although K-means++ is a powerful clustering algorithm, the whole clustering process can be improved using different heuristics. It's even possible to make the whole process entirely deterministic and therefore reproducible. This involves more advanced processes (all heuristics-based).

If you were to explore machine learning models in-depth, you could find more cases of heuristics applied in model-building. Also, many ensemble models employ heuristics in some fashion. In any case, once you gain a good grasp of heuristics, you can explore your own model-building projects using heuristics.

18.6 Summary

We looked at the potential of heuristics across different areas of data science work, such as EDA, optimization, auxiliary processes, and model-building (particularly ML-related models). Specifically, we saw how EDA has a lot to benefit from heuristics, including outlier and inlier detection, analysis of specialized variables, and new ways to measure centrality and spread in a continuous variable. What's more, we took a look at what potential optimization-related heuristics have, going further than the ones we covered in previous chapters. Also, complex problems we can tackle with a combination of optimizers may lend themselves to a heuristics-based approach for better efficiency. Additionally, we explored how we can add value to a data science project using niche heuristics. Finally, we examined how heuristics facilitate model-building in predictive models and clustering—all these possibilities appear in Figure 18.1.

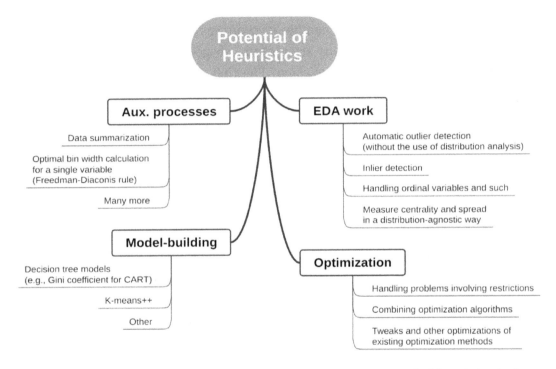

Fig. 18.1 Summary of the various possibilities regarding the potential of heuristics in data-related tasks.

Next, we'll look at heuristics through transparency. This is a very important topic in data analytics and one worth considering regardless of heuristics.

CHAPTER 19

Heuristics and Transparency

19.1 Value of transparency in data science and AI

Transparency is a characteristic of a data model or process that enables us to explain what's happening and why, or at least provide some insight into how the outputs (e.g., a model's predictions) connect to the inputs (e.g., the features). Transparency is a key aspect of data science and AI. Besides, the alternative involves *black boxes*, which are models or processes where everything that's happening in them is obscured.

The most important kind of transparency is interpretability, which involves our ability to interpret the outputs and somehow connect them to the inputs. So, if you have a binary classifier, for example, where you predict if a particular transaction is fraudulent or not, a model with interpretability would be able to explain to you which features play a role in flagging the transaction as fraudulent. Ideally, we'd be able to know how much each feature contributes to this classification. So, interpretability (and transparency) is more of a spectrum than a black-and-white situation.

Transparency is also valuable because it helps us understand the problem better and derive more value from the data. For example, if we know that features A and B are key in making accurate predictions, we focus on getting more precise values for them or more features like them (but not correlated to them). Also, if we know that features C and D don't contribute much to the model, we may decide to remove them altogether and avoid having features like that in the future. This can make the model training faster and improve the whole process.

Transparency is key in AI, too, since most data models there are opaque. This is due to their architecture, which involves a lot of obscure transformations and other processes, all of which elude our understanding. We may understand on a high level what's happening, but beyond that, we are clueless. Sometimes even the creators of these AI systems cannot explain how exactly they work and why they come up with the outputs they do. So, if we were to have more transparent AI (something often termed "eXplainable AI" or XAI), we'd have the best of both worlds: very accurate models and transparency. Unfortunately, progress in this area has been very slow. Still, it's an active area of research, even in big tech companies, showing how important it is and how much value there is in attaining some transparency in an AI-based model.

19.2 How heuristics can help with transparency

But how do heuristics fit in all this? And how can they add value? We saw that they are powerful tools for creativity, but transparency seems to be a completely different game. Still, heuristics are quite versatile, so they can add value in this area. For instance, the EDA heuristics we examined are ideal for determining which variables are more important and how they relate to the target variable when dealing with predictive analytics scenarios. This way, even if we were to use a black-box model, we could still have an idea of which features are likely to contribute to the end result since the heuristics can give us some ground truth, which will also be independent of the predictive models we use.

When we analyze the relationship between a feature and the target variable using RBC or one of the binary similarity metrics, we look at the data. Although we don't consider any data model, the latter may come up independently with this insight. The relationship preexists the modeling, so even if the model isn't transparent, our understanding of the role a feature plays will still be there regardless. This is akin to having domain knowledge, though this kind of knowledge that heuristics enable is more low-level and scalable in data analytics work.

Heuristics could also help with transparency by creating a more transparent set of meta-features. For example, current dimensionality reduction methods like autoencoders are great, but they are black boxes. If we were to use a heuristics-based approach to performing this task, the whole thing would be much more transparent. So much so that you could trace back each metafeature to its exact components, much like you can do with the PCA method. The difference here (and that's a big difference) is that if you were to use state-of-the-art heuristics, you might be able to capture non-linear relationships, too, something beyond the capabilities of PCA.

Additionally, we can modify many predictive data models to employ heuristics. If this is done properly, you may obtain a better level of transparency than what the original models yield. Of course, it would make sense to do that with models that aren't transparent already. If we were to go down the heuristics route, we could have a whole batch of data models that are both AI-based and transparent. Naturally, this is not an easy task, but no progress in the data-driven paradigm had ever been "easy". However, the more people commit to such a progressive endeavor, the easier for everyone, just like the ANN renaissance has shown us through the deep learning models.

Finally, (meta)heuristics can help us optimize the meta-parameters of a model. If we were to pay close attention to their optimal solutions, we could better understand what makes those models tick, namely, what configurations get them to work well. We can better understand how they work if they are opaque as models. This can't make them entirely transparent, but we can at least get a feel of their functionality for the data.

19.3 Building a more transparent framework for data science

If we were to put all of this understanding into practice, we'd make strides toward a more transparent framework for data science based on heuristics. After all, heuristics are part of the data-driven paradigm, which is gaining lots of ground lately and seems to be the future for advanced analytics.

Perhaps it is somewhat optimistic, but it is possible to build a transparent framework for data science under the data-driven paradigm. A framework that's not just explainable but also good at figuring out the geometry of the data and making accurate predictions. But if this were to be a real possibility for the future, perhaps we ought to understand better our past, namely the origins of our fields.

It would be interesting to delve into the history of statistics and learn about the life and works of people like Bayes and Fisher. Even if statistical models aren't as powerful or as popular as they once were, the methodical approach to data analytics that these pioneers maintained is remarkable. This was a time lacking versatile computers unless you count the crude machines Ada Lovelace and her mentor worked with as computers. So, all of the work these pioneers did was by hand. Still, they understood how data behaved and drew general inferences using just math.

What if we were to employ the same ingenuity and reasoning to the problem of data analytics using our understanding of heuristics as a starting point? Could it be that some of the metrics we now take for granted could be refined or even redefined, optimizing our approach to data? These are among the questions we ought to ask ourselves from time to time. At the very least, they can help us regain the sense of wonder that was the key motivator for many of us to pursue this field as a career.

19.4 Important considerations

To avoid misinterpretation, you need to have a solid understanding of how heuristics work. Some of these heuristics are complicated and aren't as easy to master as it first seems. They may even have been designed for a somewhat different task. Fortunately, with enough practice, you can get a good grip on them, helping make your analysis more transparent.

Additionally, you can always build your own heuristics to facilitate transparency. It's not always easy, but it's doable, and with some practice, you can do it too. If you are not a hands-on person but are still involved in data pipelines, you can leverage the help of others who have the right skill set and lead them accordingly. Transparency is a worthy goal in analytics, and if you have some ideas of heuristics that may help make it happen, it's worth pursuing them in whatever way you can.

What's more, heuristics may not be the visible part of a transparent model. Often, they lurk in the engine of that model, hidden from everyone except the people who maintain and review its codebase. That's perfectly fine since they never were the celebrities of data tools, while we praise people who use such tools or any tools creatively. The point isn't to put heuristics in the limelight. What deserves the limelight is transparency in the data models we use and the benefits of these systems for the end user.

Finally, transparency is a relative term and even if a model isn't 100% transparent, having some transparency is definitely worth it. This can help bring about more confidence in these models and the data-driven paradigm that maintains a bad reputation due to its many opaque models (mostly the ANN-based ones). Although there are use cases for such models because of the high accuracy these models yield, it's good to remember that transparency may be the next big thing in analytics and, perhaps one day, a requirement for most data models. So if heuristics can help us with this, maybe we should give them a chance and lead by example in this area.

19.5 Summary

We took a look at transparency and how heuristics can help. Transparency is very important in data science and AI. It provides a better understanding of the various models/processes and how their outputs connect to their inputs (usually features). What's more, we explored how heuristics can help with transparency to a large extent through the insights they often provide about the features and their relationships, especially when there is a target variable involved. Additionally, we looked at how building a more transparent framework for data science is a real possibility through heuristics. For this to happen, we'd need to refine and redefine many of the concepts we take for granted and which we manifest using the model-driven paradigm. Finally, we examined some important considerations about heuristics and transparency.

Next, we'll share some final thoughts on heuristics and their role in developing our creativity. We'll also talk about how we can move forward from here, armed with this know-how and the seeds of a more creative mindset.

CHAPTER 20

Final Thoughts

20.1 Heuristics and their value

All in all, we can say that the value of heuristics is two-fold: internal and external. The internal part has to do with our self-development as data professionals, particularly the honing of our creativity and our algorithmic thinking. This translates into being better equipped to find solutions to problems that often surface in our workflows and eventually save money and resources (e.g., time, computing power, memory, and hard disk space).

The latter is part of the external value of the heuristics, along with the fact that they allow us to develop different strategies for these problems and new workflows. All that can save a lot of time and effort, not just for us, but also for anyone whose work links to our data pipelines. After all, they are creativity tools, not just cool things we put together in a hackathon to hone our skills. Furthermore, these tools need to apply to all sorts of scenarios, not just the ones that brought about their existence.

20.2 Is there an end to creativity when it comes to heuristics?

You may have wondered about this, especially after delving into the specifics of heuristics and the small number of scalable heuristics. Since we don't have sufficient data, we can't find a reliable answer to this question.

If the history of invention has taught us anything, our ingenuity and creativity tend to expand as new discoveries come about. At the time of Isaac Newton, few people cared about physics and none of them could land a job or start a career in that field. Was it because there was no creativity in physics? Fortunately, Newton proved them wrong and single-handedly revamped the field of physics and made it a respectable discipline for serious scientists.

Something similar happened when a great statistics researcher came up with some new ideas that brought about the field of statistics. Perhaps this man would have been a career data analyst, but he already had a job as he was a man of the cloth. Still, Bayesian statistics remain relevant to this day, partly due to their empirical approach to analytics. These days they may even be experiencing a renaissance as more people are becoming aware of the value of data-driven data analysis. Still, in that field, creativity hadn't run out then and probably won't run out now.

Beyond these more theoretical fields, there is also engineering. At around the turn of the 20th century, there was a stagnation in applied science (engineering) as there weren't many big ideas around. At least that's what the US patent office thought as its commissioner, Henry J. Ellsworth famously reported that "Mankind has already achieved all of which it is capable. There would be no more inventions requiring patents." Fortunately, Nikola Tesla didn't take this statement seriously and literally invented what we came to know as the age of electricity and wireless communications. This happens when you rely on empirical data from experimentation powered by creativity, rather than the rumblings of some "expert" in a field.

Could heuristics be just another manifestation of the same idea of empiricism coupled with programming? Only time can tell. Until then, it doesn't hurt to act on that belief unless sufficient evidence accumulates to reject that hypothesis. Isn't that what (data) science professionals do anyway?

20.3 Heuristics as a way to develop your own creativity

Heuristics may be creativity tools, but they are also a great way to develop your own creativity. There are various ways to cultivate creativity in an empirical setting. Many people who delve in programming tend to be very creative in tackling challenging problems and coming up with elegant and swift solutions. If you have seen the function for calculating the reverse of the square root of something for the gaming company that developed Quake (where this problem needed to be solved a zillion times for each game instance as many graphics-related calculations depend on it), you would know what I mean (https://github.com/githubharald/fast_inv_sqrt and https://betterexplained.com/articles/understanding-quakes-fast-inverse-square-root). At first glance, something like this looks like magic. But if you dig into the algorithm, it's just creative engineering. Probably the programmer who came up with this solution wasn't born with this idea. If that's the case, he probably came up with it through a creative approach to this problem to optimize that function.

However, it's best to try things out yourself. Give heuristics some time and delve into them. Perhaps come up with your own heuristics whenever needed. Then see if all this process has had an impact on your creativity. At the very least, it should bring about a bit more confidence in your problem-solving endeavors. This is something subtle, so it may not register at first. However, if you have invested time and effort in such endeavors, they will pay off, even if it's not evident.

Creativity is just a way to do things unconventionally while developing novel solutions. There is no magic in it, though an outside observer may view it as something that came out of a wizard's book. Then again, everything technological that's advanced enough may look this way from outside. So, if there is nothing inherently transcendental to the creativity we encounter in the data world, perhaps it's more accessible than we think. Maybe it's just another skill we need to develop. So far, the best way we've found to develop new skills is through practice. If heuristics can provide you with a sandbox to practice this skill, then perhaps they can be a valid way to develop your creativity.

20.4 Important considerations

To better manage your expectations regarding heuristics, let's look at some final important considerations about them overall. First of all, heuristics are tools for creativity but not a substitute for creativity. In other words, they are not going to save you if you are tackling a novel problem that can only be solved through a creative approach. If all problem-solving could be outsourced to heuristics, engineers would be out of work. However, a quick look at the job market will confirm that they are still in high demand. Lately, data engineers are more in demand than data science professionals and data analysts. That's not to say that you have to be an engineer to use heuristics, but they cannot replace human ingenuity, no matter how well-made and clever they are.

The heuristics of today may seem amazing (at least to those who have developed an appreciation for this sort of stuff), but that's because the technology available to us is amazing. A few decades ago, people came up with these sorts of metrics and algorithms with the primitive machines they had at their disposal. Perhaps today's heuristics will seem like something a high school pupil of the near future would play around with because she doesn't have access to quantum computers that adults would regularly handle in that era. And probably there will be newer and better heuristics for these advanced machines.

Additionally, learning new programming languages can open up avenues for new heuristics, for example, through memory management hacks. It's no coincidence that people who speak multiple languages tend to be better at expressing themselves in their native language and communicating in general. Programming languages are not that different in that respect. Perhaps that's why good programmers tend to command a great deal of respect. So, if you don't know Julia well enough yet, it might be a good idea to learn it better. And if you do know Julia quite well, perhaps it's time to learn another high-performance language too.

Moreover, it's always good to remember there are also bad (substandard) heuristics out there. Although not entirely relevant to data work, the body mass index (BMI) is a heuristic in this category. Although it serves some purpose, it's not very good for individuals with lots of muscle mass who may be deemed overweight based on that heuristic. Cathy O'Neal explains this better in her book. In any case, heuristics are stepping stones to a solution and not works of art or something to be taken as law. Use them the best you can but remember that they may be flawed in ways that are not obvious to you, or perhaps not even to their creators.

Furthermore, a good heuristic is often as good as its implementation. So, even if the idea behind it is brilliant, it's important to pay attention as to how you implement it. Sometimes it's better to tackle it several times before you decide whether it's doable or not. Other times, it's better just to take a step back and focus on something else that's more promising. In any case, it's good to remember that many people in the past had great ideas, but they never took off because the implementation wasn't there. If you need help, it's better to ask someone since you may be better at designing a solution than implementing it (at least for now).

Finally, before you develop a new heuristic, it would be best to explore what heuristics are already out there for this task. Maybe someone else has taken a stab at that problem and come up with an algorithm that solves it adequately. So, coming up with a new method for it would be unnecessary, even if it benefits you personally. That's one of the advantages of the open-source movement and the various code repositories. So, if you wish to explore new heuristics, it would be best to start in places where others haven't done anything useful yet.

20.5 Where do we go from here in our heuristics journey?

You can do three things now to empower yourself in the heuristic journey: practice, practice, and practice. At first, you can focus on the more established heuristics before looking at the more experimental ones and making their logic familiar to yours. If they make sense and you can explain them to someone without getting a blank stare in return, all while using these heuristics yourself, they are essentially yours somehow. Then you can proceed to build your own, which will be yours 100%, at least before you put them in a public repository, in which case they will gradually become public domain.

Hacking the heuristics you know to learn more about their limitations is another strategy you can employ. After all, they are work-in-progress, so if you participate in their evolution, you need to push them to their limits. Namely, you can look at how they perform in extreme cases (e.g., large dimensionalities or large number of data points) and pinpoint potential issues they may exhibit then. Afterward, you can try to fix them whenever possible. What better way to get some skin in the game and be vested in them beyond the superficial level?

Exploring trends and possibilities in the heuristics world is another strategy you can consider. Things change rapidly in the data world, doubly so in the data-driven part of it. So, the heuristics algorithmic landscape (or algo-scape, if you will) is bound to change over time, perhaps even before this book has started to gather dust. You must develop the corresponding mindset. This way you can develop an intuition as to what's happening and anticipate the newest developments.

Heuristics can also find applications in cryptography, so if you are interested in this field and cybersecurity in general, you may want to explore that possibility too. In fact, the ectropy heuristic was developed with encryption in mind.

It's good to remember that the best heuristics are those yet to be invented. In other words, all the heuristics we've covered in this book may one day be old news as newer and better ones will come about. That's the way of things in the data world and the sooner you make peace with this, the better. However, even when all of these tools have turned into dust and air, one thing is bound to linger: the creativity impetus and the calm confidence that you can use it for problem-solving tasks. Hopefully, this can also manifest into new tools, heuristics-related or otherwise.

Finally, just like in chess, heuristics are essentially methods for obtaining useful results. As Emanuel Lasker, the longest-reigning chess world champion eloquently put it, "you should keep in mind no names, nor numbers, nor isolated incidents, not even results, but only methods. The method produces numerous results."

Glossary

A

Accuracy (Rate): a commonly used metric for evaluating a classification system, across all of the classes it predicts. It denotes the proportion of data points predicted correct. Good for balanced datasets, but inaccurate for many other cases. Accuracy is the default metric for the K-fold cross validation method.

Algorithm: a step-by-step procedure for calculations and logical operations. In a data science / AI setting, algorithms can be designed to facilitate machine learning and acquire knowledge by themselves, rather than relying on hard-coded rules. Algorithms often rely on heuristics for their evaluations and decisions.

Area Under Curve (AUC) metric: a heuristic metric for a binary classifier's performance, based on the ROC curve. It can takes into account the confidence of the classifier when available and is generally considered a more robust performance index than accuracy, for example. AUC takes values between 0 and 1 (inclusive) and a higher value is better. Generally, values around 0.5, or anything less than that, are considered bad.

Artificial Intelligence (AI): a field of computer science dealing with the emulation of human intelligence using computer systems and its applications on a variety of domains. The application of AI on data science is noteworthy and an important factor in the field, especially since the 2000s. AI comes in various shapes and forms, yet it is closely linked to heuristics.

Artificial Neural Network (ANN): a graph-based artificial intelligence system, implementing the universal approximator idea. Although ANNs have started as a machine learning system, focusing on predictive analytics, they have expanded over the years to include a large variety of tasks. ANNs consist of a series of nodes called neurons, which are organized in layers. The first layer corresponds to all the inputs, the final layer to all the outputs, and the intermediary layers to a series of metafeatures the ANN creates, each having a corresponding weight. ANNs are stochastic in nature so every time they are trained over a set of data, the weights are noticeably different.

Autoencoder: a specialized ANN that attempts to develop a lower dimensionality representation of the data. Autoencoders are often used for developing new data points too (data synthesis).

B

Bias (of a model): a key characteristic of a predictive model relating to its performance. High bias means that a model is off consistently, while low bias means that it's more accurate on average. Bias is a key component of a model's performance, and it's linked to its variance in the bias-variance trade-off.

Bias-variance trade-off: a law of sorts describing the performance of a model. According to it, if a model's bias increases, its variance decreases, and vice-versa. The bias-variance trade-off plays an important role in model optimization, for all predictive analytics models.

Black box: a predictive analytics model or process that is not in any way transparent or comprehensible in how it arrives to its predictions. Many machine learning models are black boxes, contrary to Statistical models that are generally transparent.

C

Centroid: the center of a cluster of data points. The coordinates of the centroids are usually among the outputs of a clustering method.

Chromosome: in the genetic algorithms (GAs) framework, this is a potential solution. Each chromosome consists of genes, which are parts of the solution. During mating, two chromosomes merge and a new pair of chromosomes come about, each consisting of different elements of the parent chromosomes. Chromosomes are an essential part of solving optimization problems with GAs and special care needs to be taken as to how they encode a potential solution.

Classification: a very popular data science methodology, under the predictive analytics umbrella. Classification aims to solve the problem of assigning a label (aka class) to a data point, based on pre-existing knowledge of categorized data, available in the training set.

Classifier: a predictive analytics system geared towards classification problems.

Clustering: a data science methodology involving finding groups in a given dataset, usually using the distances among the data points as a similarity metric. Clustering is an unsupervised learning methodology. As a problem, clustering is NP-hard, and it's frequently tackled with heuristics and metaheuristics.

Codebook: *see notebook (for coding).*

Collinearity: the state of a feature set whereby two or more features correlated strongly to each other. Collinearity can be an issue with some data models, and it is usually handled with dimensionality reduction.

Confidence: a metric that aims to reflect the probability of another metric being correct. Usually it takes values between 0 and 1 (inclusive). Confidence is linked to Statistics, but it lends itself to heuristics and machine learning systems too, since it is entirely independent as a concept. Confidence is particularly important in classification since many machine learning models use it for their final decision, i.e., which one the dominant class of the prediction is.

Confusion matrix: a k-by-k matrix depicting the hits and misses of a classifier, for a problem involving k classes. For a binary problem (involving 2 classes only), the matrix consists of various combinations of hits (trues) and misses (falses) referred to as true positives (cases of value 1 predicted as 1), true negatives (cases of value 0 predicted as 0), false positives (cases of value 0 predicted as 1), and false negatives (cases of value 1 predicted as 0). The confusion matrix is the basis of most evaluation metrics relevant to classification.

Constraints (in optimization algorithms): the restrictions the variables of the optimization problem are subject to, which need to be respected by the optimization algorithm involved. Constraints take the form of mathematical equations.

Correlation (coefficient): a metric of how closely related two continuous variables are, in a linear manner.

Cost function: a function for evaluating the amount of damage the total of all misclassifications amount to, based on individual costs preassigned to different kinds of errors. A cost function is a popular heuristic metric for measuring performance in complex classification problems and it relies on the confusion matrix for its key variables.

Curse of dimensionality: see *dimensionality curse*.

Creativity: the ability to come up with novel and oftentimes efficient solutions to problems, or ideas in general. Creativity in data science is quite hands-on and involves the use of various tools, such as heuristics.

Crossover: in genetic algorithms, it is an operator whereby two chromosomes merge to yield offspring. During this mating process, genes of the two parents cross over and combine to form the new chromosomes that will be part of the next generation.

D

Data analytics: a general term to describe the field involving data analysis as its main component. Data analytics is more general than data science, although people in the business world often use the two terms interchangeably.

Data drift: the phenomenon whereby the data used for training and testing a model is significantly different to the data used once the model is deployed. Data drift can cause performance issues and eventually make the model obsolete if left unmaintained.

Data engineering: the part of the data science pipeline where data is acquired, cleaned, and processed, so that it is ready to be used in a data model. Most modern predictive models (e.g., AI-based ones) don't require a lot of data engineering as they can work on cruder forms of data all the same.

Data exploration: the part of the data science pipeline where the various variables are examined using statistics and data visualization, in order to understand it better and work out the best ways to tackle it in the stages that follow.

Data model: a data science module processing and/or predicting some piece of information, using existing data, after the latter has been preprocessed and made ready for this task. Data models add value and are comprised of non-trivial procedures. In AI, data models are usually sophisticated systems making use of several data-driven processes under the hood.

Data point: a single row in a dataset, corresponding to a single record of a database.

Data science: the interdisciplinary field undertaking data analytics work on all kinds of data, with a focus on big data, for the purpose of mining insights and/or building data products. Data science includes machine learning as well as other data analytics frameworks.

Dataset: the data available to be used in a data analytics project, in the form of a table or a matrix. A dataset may need some work before it is ready for being used in a data model, though in many machine learning models, you can use it as is.

Density: the concept of how crowded a particular part of the dataset is, or even the whole dataset as a whole. Density is evaluated through specialized advanced heuristics and can be very useful in EDA work as well as some data models. Since density heuristics work with distances, it's best to apply them on normalized data.

Deterministic: a process that always yields the same result for the same outputs. For example, all descriptive statistics methods are deterministic, though most machine learning ones are not. A process that is not deterministic is usually referred to as stochastic.

Dimensionality (of a dataset): the number of variables / features in the dataset. The higher the dimensionality, the more complex the dataset and the higher the chances of collinearities in it.

Dimensionality curse: the highly problematic situation whereby models and metrics fail due to the large number of dimensions and its effect on any distance or similarity metrics involved. The curse of dimensionality is apparent in any transductive algorithm and most distance-related heuristics.

Dimensionality reduction: the process of reducing the number of features in a dataset, typically through the merging of the original features in a more compact form (feature fusion), or through the discarding of the less information-rich features (feature selection). A commonly used method for dimensionality reduction is principal components analysis (PCA). Two popular data-driven dimensionality reduction methods are T-SNE and UMAP.

Distance: how close or far two points are in a feature space. Although often we use the Euclidean distance metric to calculate distance, there are several other metrics too, which may be more robust against the high dimensionality issue (aka, the curse of dimensionality). Distance is essential in many heuristics, particularly in data-related work.

Documentation: any relevant material (usually text) that accompanies some algorithm or metric. This may include examples of its usage, limitations, and known bugs in the current implementation of it. Heuristics typically need documentation more than any other algorithm or metric, since there is usually not much theory behind them.

E

Ectropy: a heuristic metric for measuring the order of a variable or dataset. Ectropy is supplementary to entropy and relatively easier to work with. The ectropy we refer to in this book takes values between 0 and 1, inclusive.

Embedding: a low-dimensional representation of a given set of data. Embeddings are quite common in dimensionality reduction systems, particularly machine learning ones (e.g. Isomap and autoencoders). Embeddings are often referred to as metafeatures.

Ensemble: "The process by which multiple models, such as classifiers or experts, are strategically generated and combined to solve a particular computational intelligence problem. Ensemble learning is primarily used to improve the (classification, prediction, function approximation, etc.) performance of a model, or reduce the likelihood of an unfortunate selection of a poor one." (Dr. Robi Polikar). Ensembles are usually black boxes. In any case, ensembles regularly make use of one or more heuristics to better leverage the data models or **optimizers** they have as components.

Entropy: a heuristic metric for measuring disorder in a variable or dataset. Entropy is based on probabilities and takes values between 0 and infinity. Entropy is more established than ectropy, and it's a fundamental concept in Information Theory.

Error rate: the counterpart of accuracy rate, as a performance metric for classification systems. It denotes the proportion of data points predicted wrong. Error rate works well for balanced datasets, and it's complementary to the accuracy rate: $ER = 1 - AR$.

Exploratory Data Analysis (EDA): part of the data science pipeline that involves exploring the data at hand and understanding the variables involved. EDA is essential as it provides valuable insights about the dataset and helps drive the development of data models. If done properly, EDA heavily relies on heuristics.

F

F1-score heuristic: aka F1 metric, a popular performance metric for classification systems, defined as the harmonic mean of precision and recall, and just like them, corresponds to a particular class. In cases of unbalanced datasets, it is more meaningful than accuracy rate. F1 belongs to a family of similar metrics each one being a function of precision (P) and recall (R) in the form $F_\beta = (1 + \beta^2) (P * R) / (\beta^2 P + R)$, where β is a coefficient related to importance of precision in the particular aggregation metric F_β. For the F1 metric β takes the value of 1 (i.e., precision is equally important to recall).

False Negative: in a binary classification problem, it is a data point of class 1, predicted as class 0. See confusion matrix for more context.

False Positive: in a binary classification problem, it is a data point of class 0, predicted as class 1. See confusion matrix for more context.

Feature: a processed variable capable of being used in a data science model, particularly a predictive analytics one. Features are generally the columns of a dataset.

Feature engineering: the process of creating new features, either directly from the data available, or via the processing of existing features. Feature engineering is part of data engineering, in the data science process.

Feature fusion: see fusion.

Feature selection: the data science process according to which the dimensionality of a dataset is reduced through the selection of the most promising features and the discarding of the less promising ones. How promising a feature is depends on how well it can help predict the target variable and is related to how information-rich it is.

Field: a discipline or subject. This book is about the field of data science as well as that of artificial intelligence. Heuristics are part of these fields too, under the data-driven paradigm.

Fitness function: an essential part of most artificial intelligence systems, particularly optimization related ones. It depicts how close the system is getting to the desired outcome and helps it adjust its course accordingly. In most AI systems the fitness function represents an error or some form of cost, which needs to be minimized, though in the general case it can be anything and depending on the problem, it may need to be maximized. The fitness function of an AI system can be seen as a specialized heuristic metric.

FOSS: Free and Open-Source Software. This includes any piece of software whose licensing is free (e.g., under CC license) and whose source code is available to everyone. This allows FOSS to be improved by anyone having the programming skills to fork the original commit and improve its functionality or even add new features to it. The Julia programming language is FOSS, while all of its libraries and many of the scripts developed on it are FOSS too.

Functionality (of a heuristic): the algorithm that describes how the outputs of that heuristics are obtained by processing its inputs. Figuring out the functionality of a heuristic is essential in making it a viable tool and writing code that tackles its objectives.

Fusion: usually used in conjunction with feature (e.g., feature fusion), this relates to the merging of a set of features into a single metafeature that encapsulates all, or at least most, of the information in these features. This is a popular method of dimensionality reduction, and it is an integral part of every deep learning system.

G

Gene: in genetic algorithms (GAs), a gene is part of a chromosome (potential solution to the optimization problem). Genes are passed down to the next generation through the mating process and the crossover operator.

Generalization: a key characteristic of a data science model, where the system is able to handle data beyond its training set reliably. A proxy to good generalization is similar performance between the training set and a testing set, as well as consistency among different training-testing set partitions of the whole dataset.

Generation: in GAs, an iteration of the optimization algorithm.

Genetic Algorithms (GAs): a family of optimization algorithms that rely heavily on heuristics and are stochastic in nature. GAs are ideal for combination-related problems as well as problems related to graphs.

Gini index: a heuristic used in decision trees, for measuring the impurity of a dataset as well as that of a given feature. Gini index is applicable in classification problems.

H

Harmonic mean: a measure of centrality that applies to positive non-zero numbers and which tends to be closer to the smaller ones. Harmonic mean is almost always less than the arithmetic mean (conventional average) and it's a very useful heuristic in many scenarios. The F1 metric is an example of the harmonic mean of two numbers (in that case, precision and recall values).

Heuristic: an empirical metric or algorithm/function that aims to provide some useful tool or insight, to facilitate a method or project of data science or artificial intelligence. Heuristics are entirely data-driven and focus on performing a very specific task in an efficient and scalable manner.

I

Information: any useful signal in a piece of data that can be communicated in other means. Information can also be seen as distilled data and is more high-level than data and closer to our understanding. From a technical standpoint, information is the useful aspects of a signal or transmission, something studied by the Information Theory developed by Claude Shannon. Information is related to heuristics through specialized metrics such as entropy.

Inliers: data points that are considered to be too far away from the rest of the points in the data, while still being within its limits (e.g., random point in between two groups of points). Inliers are often classified as noise and are usually omitted or replaced in the data engineering phase of the pipeline.

Insight: a non-obvious and useful piece of information deriving from the use of a data science model on some data. Insights are key deliverables in a data science project and are sometimes the product of specialized heuristics.

Interpretability: the ability to more thoroughly understand a data model's outputs and derive how they relate to its inputs (features). Lack of interpretability is an issue for deep learning systems as well as many machine learning systems in general. We often use interpretability and transparency interchangeably.

J

Julia: a modern programming language of the functional programming paradigm, comprising characteristics for both high-level and low-level languages. Its ease of use, high speed, scalability, and sufficient amount of packages, make it a robust language well-suited for data science. After v. 1.0 of the language was released, it has been officially production-ready in a wide variety of organizations.

K

K-fold Cross Validation: a fundamental data science experiment technique for building a model and ensuring that it has a reliable generalization potential. K-fold cross validation is used in combination with a performance metric (such as accuracy rate or mean square error) or any model-related heuristic (e.g., F1 score, RBC, and Area Under Curve).

K-means: a popular clustering method based on distances among the data points involved. Its key parameter, K, corresponds to the number of clusters we wish to have in the clustering process.

KISS heuristic rule: a guideline of sorts in graphics design and possibly other disciplines, where the practitioner is advised to "keep it simple, silly" so that the end-result isn't too complex or heavy. The KISS rule applies to the development of heuristics too, perhaps more than any other data science and AI related project.

L

Labels: a set of values corresponding to the points of a dataset, providing information about the dataset's structure. The latter takes the form of classes, often linked to classification applications. The variable containing the labels is usually the target variable of the dataset.

M

Machine Learning (ML): a set of algorithms and programs that aim to process data without relying on statistical methods. ML is generally faster and some methods of it are significantly more accurate than the corresponding statistical ones, while the assumptions they make about the data are fewer. There is a noticeable overlap between ML and artificial intelligence systems designed for data science.

Mapping: the process of connecting a variable or a set of variables, to a variable we are trying to predict (aka target variable). Mappings can be analytical using a mathematical function, or not, such as employing a set of rules, or a network of functions, as in the case of an artificial neural network. Mappings are inherent in every data model.

Markdown (language): a scripting language for formatting text. Although there is no need to know markdown to use coding notebooks, it's often very useful as it allows you full control of how the text is formatted. See appendix B for more information on how it facilitates Neptune notebooks.

Mean Square Error (MSE): a popular performance metric used for regression problems. It involves taking the difference between the target variable and the predicted values of the target variable, squaring it, and then taking the average of it. The model having the smallest such error is considered the better one, in the majority of cases. MSE can be seen as a kind of heuristic metric.

Metafeatures (aka super features or synthetic features): high quality features that encapsulate larger amounts of information, usually represented in a series of conventional features. Metafeatures are either synthesized in an artificial intelligence system, or created through dimensionality reduction. Generally, a metafeature has a stronger predictive potential than each one of the features it derives from. Heuristics can be a powerful tool in developing useful metafeatures.

Metaheuristic: according to Sörensen and Glover, a metaheuristic is a high-level problem-independent algorithmic framework that provides a set of guidelines / strategies for developing heuristic optimization algorithms. This makes metaheuristics essential in certain AI-related applications, which can also be useful in data science. All optimization algorithms described in this book are essentially metaheuristics.

Metric: any kind of mathematical construct designed for measuring something. Usually metrics relate to a variable, a dataset, a function, or a model. Heuristics are often used as metrics.

Model: any kind of mathematical construct for performing a mapping efficiently and with a measurable performance. Most models we deal with in data science involve the use of data as both inputs and ground truth. These are referred to as data models.

Model Maintenance: the process of updating or even upgrading a data model, as new data becomes available or as the assumptions of the problem change.

Mutation: an operator in genetic algorithms, whereby a single chromosome changes slightly in some part of it, to make the population (genome) more diverse.

N

Neptune: a code notebook environment, similar to Pluto and Jupyter, but geared towards Julia specifically. Much like Jupyter, Neptune doesn't care about the order the cells of the notebook are executed in, while at the same time it's quite lightweight, like Pluto. The notebook files Neptune handles have the .jl extension and can be run just like regular Julia scripts, using the Julia program. Although Neptune is a fork of the Pluto notebook, its functionality is significantly better, and it's well-suited for data science work.

Noise: all the parts of the dataset that don't add any value to data science work due to their random nature. Noise is usually handled in the data engineering phase and is in contrast with the signal of the dataset.

Normalization: the process of transforming a variable so that it is of the same scale as the other variables in a dataset. This is done through statistical methods primarily and is part of the data engineering stage of the data science pipeline. The most common normalization methods are min-max (where the minimum of a variable is made to be 0.0

and the maximum 1.0) and standardization (where the mean of a variable is made to be 0.0 and the standard deviation 1.0). Normalization is essential for the proper function of various heuristics, particularly distance-based ones.

Notebook (for coding): an interacting coding environment that blends HTML, CSS, and a programming language, like Julia. Coding notebooks are very popular in Analytics work and work with various web browsers, by creating a web server on the computer they are run. You don't need an internet connection to use such a notebook, unless that notebook lives on the cloud (e.g., Google's Colab). Although Jupyter is the most common coding notebook out there, for Julia users there are other options, such as Neptune and Pluto.

NP-hard problem: any problem that is at least as hard as an NP-problem. Chances are, however, that an NP-hard problem is going to be harder. NP-hard problems are ideally tackled with metaheuristics. NP-hard problems tend not to scale very well.

NP-problem: a problem that is solvable in polynomial time by a nondeterministic Turing machine. NP-problems tend to scale quite well.

O

Objective (of a heuristic): what the heuristic attempts to accomplish. This could be something simple like gauging the information content of a variable, to something more complex, like figuring out how peculiar each of the data points in a dataset are.

Objective function: the function that needs to be optimized, in an optimization problem. Often it is referred to as fitness function.

Optimization: an artificial intelligence process, aimed at finding the best value of a function (usually referred to as the fitness function) given a set of restrictions. Optimization is key in all modern data science systems, particularly machine learning ones. Although there are deterministic optimization algorithms out there, most of the modern algorithms are stochastic. The latter make use of heuristics in one way or another (metaheuristics in particular).

Optimizer: a (usually AI based) system designed to perform optimization. Many modern optimizers make use of heuristics and are even metaheuristics themselves.

Outliers: data points that are considered to be too far away from the rest of the points in the data. Outliers are classified as noise and are typically omitted or replaced in the data engineering phase of the pipeline.

Overfitting: the case whereby a model is too specialized to a particular dataset, yielding excessive variance. Its main characteristic is good performance for the training set and poor performance for any other dataset. Overfitting is a characteristic of an overly complex model.

P

Parallelism: the use of parallel computing, either through multi-threading or cluster computing, to facilitate and speed up certain processes. Parallelism is more or less essential in various AI-related applications, including optimization ensembles (or even regular optimizers, for that matter).

Particle Swarm Optimization (PSO): a swarm-based optimization algorithm that's based on certain heuristics. PSO is ideal for problems containing continuous variables and is stochastic in nature.

Performance metric: a heuristic geared towards evaluating the performance of a data model. Performance metrics are an essential part of validating a model, making sure it is ready for being put into production. Also, every methodology has its own performance metrics. Popular performance metrics for Classification are Accuracy and F1 score, while for Regression the Mean Square Error is usually used. Most performance metrics are essentially heuristics designed for that purpose.

Pipeline: also known as workflow, it is a conceptual process involving a variety of steps, each one of which can consist of several other processes. A pipeline is essential for organizing the tasks needed to perform any complex procedure (often non-linear) and is very applicable in data science (this application is known as the data science pipeline).

Population: in genetic algorithm, this refers to the collection of all chromosomes. The term genome is used sometimes too.

Precision: a performance metric for classification systems, focusing on a particular class. It is defined as the ratio of the true positives of that class over the total number of predictions related to that class. Precision is complementary to Recall as a performance metric for classification. The combination of these two metrics yields a series of useful heuristics, the best known of which is the F1-score.

Predictive analytics: a set of methodologies of data analytics, related to the prediction of certain variables. It includes a variety of techniques such as classification, regression, time-series analysis, and more. Predictive analytics are a key part of data science and one that adds the most value in data science projects.

Preprocessing: any task or set of tasks that are performed in the data engineering stage, to ensure that the dataset is ready for a data model. Preprocessing is usually essential, especially when the target variable has some kind of imbalance. Heuristics can help a great deal in preprocessing.

Problem: anything that manifests as a blockage in your work or in the development of a solution such as a data product. Problems come in various shapes and forms and tend to be domain-specific. For certain problems, we have some formula or process (algorithm) that can help us solve them. For everything else, we have heuristics.

R

Recall: a performance metric for classification systems, focusing on a particular class. It is defined as the ratio of the true positives of that class over the total number of data points related to that class. Recall is complementary to Precision as a performance metric for classification. The combination of these two metrics yields a series of useful heuristics, the best known of which is the F1-score.

Robust (model): a state whereby a model is not overfit, yielding a consistent performance across different data samples. Robust models are considered reliable enough to be used in production.

ROC analysis: short for Receiver Operating Characteristics analysis, an evaluation method for binary classifiers, examining how the False Positive Rate and the True Positive Rate (Recall) relate with each other. The result of this analysis usually takes the form of a curve (aka ROC curve) while the area under that curve can be used as a holistic evaluation metric (aka AUC). Yet, even without the AUC metric, the ROC analysis is useful as it examines how the different values for the decision threshold (often depicted as λ) affect the outcome of the classifier, helping us decide what the best trade-off between FP and FN is, for the problem at hand.

ROC curve: a curve representing the trade-off between true positives and false positives for a binary classification problem, useful for evaluating the classifier used. The ROC curve is usually a zigzag line, depicting the true positive rate for each false positive rate value. The area under the curve is also used as an evaluation metric, namely the AUC heuristic.

S

Sample: a limited portion of the data available, useful for building a model, and (ideally) representative of the population it belongs to.

Sampling: the process of acquiring a sample of a population using a specialized technique. Sampling is very important to be done properly, to ensure that the resulting sample is representative of the population studied. Sampling needs to be unbiased, something usually accomplished by making it random. Nevertheless, there are way to perform sampling deterministically, with certain heuristics.

Scope: a key characteristic of a heuristic involving its functionality. The scope of a heuristic is intimately linked to its usability and the breadth of use cases it can handle. Scope is also closely linked to the objectives of the heuristic.

Sensitivity Analysis: the process of establishing how stable a result is or how prone a model's performance is to change, if the initial data is different. It involves several methods, such as re-sampling, "what if" questions, etc. For binary classification problems it involves additional tools such as ROC analysis.

Signal: the underlying gist of a dataset, which depicts the information within the data at hand. The signal is not easily measurable, and it's often contradicted to the noise of the data.

Similarity metrics: all the different (mostly heuristic) metrics that help us assess the similarity of two variables or data points. Cosine similarity, for example, takes into account the angle of the vectors corresponding to what we are comparing (e.g., two data points in a high-dimensionality space) in relation to a reference point (the point where all the axes meet). Due to its nature, this metric isn't influenced by the dimensionality of the space since it doesn't employ distance calculations.

Solution: a value or collection of values that solves a given problem. In software engineering, a solution takes the form of a complete piece of software, while in data-related disciplines, a particular collection of data (sometimes expressible graphically). Although in some domains an accurate value is required, more often than not, a close-enough approximation is a viable option too. Solutions tend to come about using specialized algorithms and/or heuristics.

Solution space: the space where all possible solutions of a problem dwell. Traversing the solution space efficiently is usually accomplished through the use of some heuristic that speeds up the process.

Stochastic: something that is probabilistic in nature (i.e., not deterministic). Stochastic processes are common in most artificial intelligence system and other advanced machine learning systems.

Subfield: a partition of a field. Optimization is a subfield of AI and Statistics a subfield of Mathematics. Although heuristics aren't regarded a subfield yet, they are an important component of data analytics, particularly in the data-driven paradigm.

Swarm: the collection of all potential solutions (aka particles) in a certain kind of optimizers, such as PSO.

T

Target variable: the variable of a dataset that is the target of a predictive analytics system, such as a classification or a regression system.

Testing set: the part of the dataset that is used for testing a predictive analytics model after it has been trained and before it is deployed. The testing set usually corresponds to a small portion of the original dataset.

Tool (for data science and AI): any method or model that helps us with our data science projects. This can be something that provides us with predictions, confidence evaluation, performance evaluation, and any insights that help us understand the inner workings of the processes involved (transparency). Heuristics are great tools for that and for expressing our creativity.

Training algorithm: the algorithm used for training a deep learning system (or a predictive analytics model in general). It entails figuring out which nodes to keep and what weights their connections have, to obtain a good generalization for the problem at hand. Back-propagation is an established training algorithm, suitable for various kinds of artificial neural networks, including deep learning systems.

Training set: the part of the dataset that is used for training a predictive analytics model before it is tested and deployed. The training set usually corresponds to the largest portion of the original dataset.

Transparency (in a data model or process): an important characteristic of a model or process, related to its ability to explain how it arrives to a particular conclusion as well as how confident it is about its predictions. Lack of transparency is often referred to as being a "black box." Transparency is often referred to as interpretability.

Transductive (model or heuristic): making use of direct reasoning, usually through a distance metric. The transductive approach is complementary to the traditional inductive and deductive ones.

True Negative: in a binary classification problem, it is a data point of class 0, predicted as such. See confusion matrix for more context.

True Positive: in a binary classification problem, it is a data point of class 1, predicted as such. See confusion matrix for more context.

U

Underfitting: the state of a model whereby it has insufficient variance, leading to substandard performance, consistently. Underfitting is a sign of an overly simplistic model characterized by high bias.

Usability: a key characteristic of a heuristic that has to do with how it is perceived and utilized by the user. Just like scope, usability is linked to the heuristic's functionality.

V

Variable: a column in a dataset, be it in a matrix or a data frame. Variables are usually transformed into features, after some data engineering is performed on them.

Variance (of a model): a key characteristic of a predictive model relating to its performance. A model of high variance is bound to be unstable and as a result unreliable. Low variance is generally better, though the model's overall performance must take into account its bias too.

Variance (of a variable): a metric related to how the values of the variable vary, in relation to its average. Variance is important in most statistical models as well as a metric for describing a variable.

W

Workflow: *see pipeline*.

Key Components of a Heuristic

1. Aim/Objectives

This is the most important part, and it's closely linked to the *problem* the heuristic tries to solve along with any restrictions that are in place. The latter is particularly relevant in optimization problems, as well as any data-related problem that's complex enough.

The aim is the general goal of the heuristic and it's important to have it clearly stated when you embark on a heuristic-related journey. In more complex situations, the aim of the heuristic is often expressed as a series of objectives. These are also related to the outputs of the heuristic though they may also be intermediary steps towards a single output. When tackling a problem, the objectives may be linked to specific solutions of the problem or different stages of the solution. It's often useful to write down the objectives of a heuristic when setting out to create it.

2. Functionality

This is in essence the algorithm of the heuristic, i.e., the way of obtaining the outputs using its inputs. A heuristic's functionality is essential to figure out since it gives the heuristic its usefulness and enables it to take more tangible forms, e.g., a function in a programming language. Because of this fact, it's also the most challenging part of a heuristic, when developing a new one. Having a clear idea of the other aspects of the heuristic helps significantly though.

Note that for the more complex heuristics out there (including most of the metaheuristics), functionality involves the use of auxiliary functions that facilitate or even undertake altogether the heuristic's various processes. Having a clear idea of a heuristic's functionality enables us to write clean and efficient code to implement it. It also helps, especially for the more complex heuristics, to create a flowchart of their whole functionality along with a list of all the essential auxiliary functions to be used.

3. Parameters, Outputs, and Usability (as well as Scope)

These aspects of a heuristic are also important as they help make the heuristic more concrete and usable to other people. Also, when developing a new heuristic, they help us understand it better and implement it more efficiently.

The scope, in particular, is important for managing expectations and defining the applicability of the heuristic. This involves things like what variable(s) the heuristic is applicable on, what problems it can tackle, and what its limitations are. Having a clear understanding of the scope is essential for using the heuristic effectively and justifying its use. When creating a new heuristic, scope is also important as it helps us limit the problem we are trying to solve and therefore solve it more efficiently.

Regarding the parameters of the heuristic, these are also important as they make its functionality more concrete. In essence, they are the inputs of the heuristic and play an important role in how it tackles the problem at hand. Some of its parameters involve the data it processes (e.g., a subset of variables from a dataset, or an objective function it tries to optimize), while others involve certain aspects of the processes involved in it. Optimizing the non-data-related parameters of a heuristic can sometimes be a problem in itself, which is why heuristics with few such parameters are often preferable. However, for a heuristic to be more applicable to various problems (i.e., have a larger scope), some non-data-related parameters are necessary.

As for the heuristic's outputs, these are in essence the potential solutions to the problem the heuristic tackles. In optimization, this takes the form of a set of variable values which either maximize or minimize the objective function, all while respecting any restrictions the problem entails. Additionally, the outputs of a heuristic may include additional information, which may be useful for other processes. The outputs are frequently a good place to start when designing a heuristic, so that you have a clear idea of what you expect to get out of it.

4. Important notes

Heuristics are always limited and oftentimes inaccurate. However, they are a good first attempt to tackling a problem and may provide insights that can help solve it. Sometimes, a heuristic metric can be the basis for a metaheuristic that solves the problem thoroughly (within the predefined scope). So, when you develop a heuristic, remember that you are not competing with the state-of-the-art solutions out there.

Also, through the development and implementation of heuristics you cultivate your creativity and gather useful experience in problem-solving. Additionally, sometimes a heuristic may not be so impressive or a good value-add unless it's utilized with the right algorithm (wrapper function), so it's good to be mindful of this too. Finally, it's always important to read any documentation a heuristic has and write such a piece of text when developing a new heuristic.

Installing and Using Neptune on Your Computer

1. Installing the software

First of all, make sure you have Julia installed on your computer. You can find the latest versions of the language at the official website, with some comments as to how to make it work on your machine: https://julialang.org/downloads

Next, you need to ensure that you have the *Neptune* package installed. You can do that by following these steps, when you are in the Julia environment (i.e., you can see the *julia>* prompt):

1. Press] to change the prompt from *julia>* to *(@v1.x) pkg>* (this is the package manager). You don't need to press enter for this.

2. Type "add Neptune" and press enter. This may take a few seconds, while it installs and possibly updates your repository, to make sure that Neptune can run smoothly. You will need an internet connection for this.

2. Running Neptune on Julia

To run Neptune you need to do the following steps:

1. Run Julia.

2. Type "using Neptune" and press enter. This should load the package into memory.

Fig. B.1 Welcome screen of Neptune notebook.

3. Type "Neptune.run()" and press enter. This should open a window or tab on your browser where the Neptune main screen will appear. Note that Neptune works best with Chrome-based browsers. If you have a different browser as a default, it's best to type "Neptune.run(;launch_browser=false)" instead and copy the link that Neptune provides to your browser manually.

4. Select one of the sample codebooks to open, or create a new one. Alternatively, you can open one of the codebooks provided with this book (they all have a relevant name that points to the fact that they are Neptune notebooks rather than conventional Julia script files).

5. Once you are done with your work, you can exit Neptune by pressing Control and C on your Julia window. You can also close the corresponding window/tab on your browser, since you won't be able to do much with it once the Neptune package isn't active.

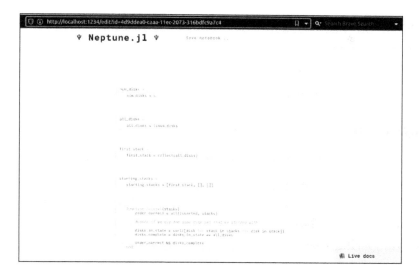

Fig. B.2 Sample Neptune notebook.

The commands you can use in the Neptune codebook cells are more or less the same as those in Julia. However, for writing text, you need to use the markdown command as follows:

Md"""some text and formatting characters"""

If you are unfamiliar with markdown, you can consult this reference guide here: https://www.markdownguide.org/basic-syntax

3. Additional material for learning this software

For a quick reference to the Julia language, you can make use of this webpage: https://juliadocs.github.io/Julia-Cheat-Sheet

For the latest documentation on Neptune, you can check out its official Github webpage: https://github.com/compleathorseplayer/Neptune.jl

Note that Neptune is heavily based on the Pluto notebook, which although great, isn't very suitable for data analytics work. Still, it's well-documented and can be a great place to start when learning Neptune. For a quick overview of the Pluto commands you can refer to this webpage: https://github.com/fonsp/Pluto.jl/wiki/%F0%9F%94%8E-Basic-Commands-in-Pluto

4. Important notes

Although you could edit a Neptune notebook through a text editor (e.g., Atom), it's best if you didn't unless you really know what you are doing. These codebook files are very sensitive and may not work properly if you change them. For example, each cell has its own unique reference ID which is included as a comment. Tampering with that may break the notebook.

Additionally, for Neptune to work properly, it requires a couple of packages to be running, which you can see in every Neptune codebook file, so make sure that you keep them around in your Julia package library, even if you don't use them elsewhere.

What's more, once you make some changes to a Neptune notebook, it's good practice to "submit all changes" to it, by clicking the corresponding link on the top of the notebook, before shutting down that process (usually from the terminal or from Julia). If you don't do that, you risk losing all your work (at least the latest part) upon closing the Neptune notebook tab or window, on your browser.

Finally, unlike Jupyter, Neptune doesn't keep the outputs in the notebook files, not even the text cells. So, if you want to showcase a notebook that has been executed, you will need to export it as a PDF or an HTML file.

Fig. B.3 Export options for a Neptune notebook

Index

www.ingramcontent.com/pod-product-compliance
Lightning Source LLC
Chambersburg PA
CBHW080525060326
40690CB00022B/5032